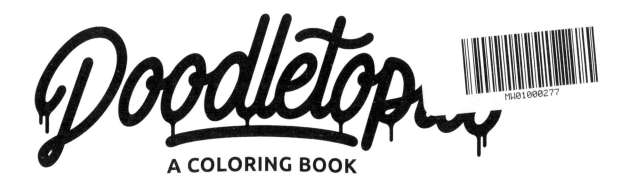

A COLORING BOOK

Vexx.

A TARCHERPERIGEE BOOK

tarcherperigee

AN IMPRINT OF PENGUIN RANDOM HOUSE LLC
PENGUINRANDOMHOUSE.COM

TARCHERPERIGEE WITH TP COLOPHON IS A REGISTERED TRADEMARK OF PENGUIN RANDOM HOUSE LLC

MOST TARCHERPERIGEE BOOKS ARE AVAILABLE AT SPECIAL QUANTITY DISCOUNTS FOR BULK
PURCHASE FOR SALES PROMOTIONS, PREMIUMS, FUNDRAISING, AND EDUCATIONAL NEEDS.
SPECIAL BOOKS OR BOOK EXCERPTS ALSO CAN BE CREATED TO FIT SPECIFIC NEEDS.
FOR DETAILS, WRITE SPECIALMARKETS@PENGUINRANDOMHOUSE.COM.

TRADE PAPERBACK ISBN: 9780593713389

PRINTED IN THE UNITED STATES OF AMERICA
1   3   5   7   9   10   8   6   4   2

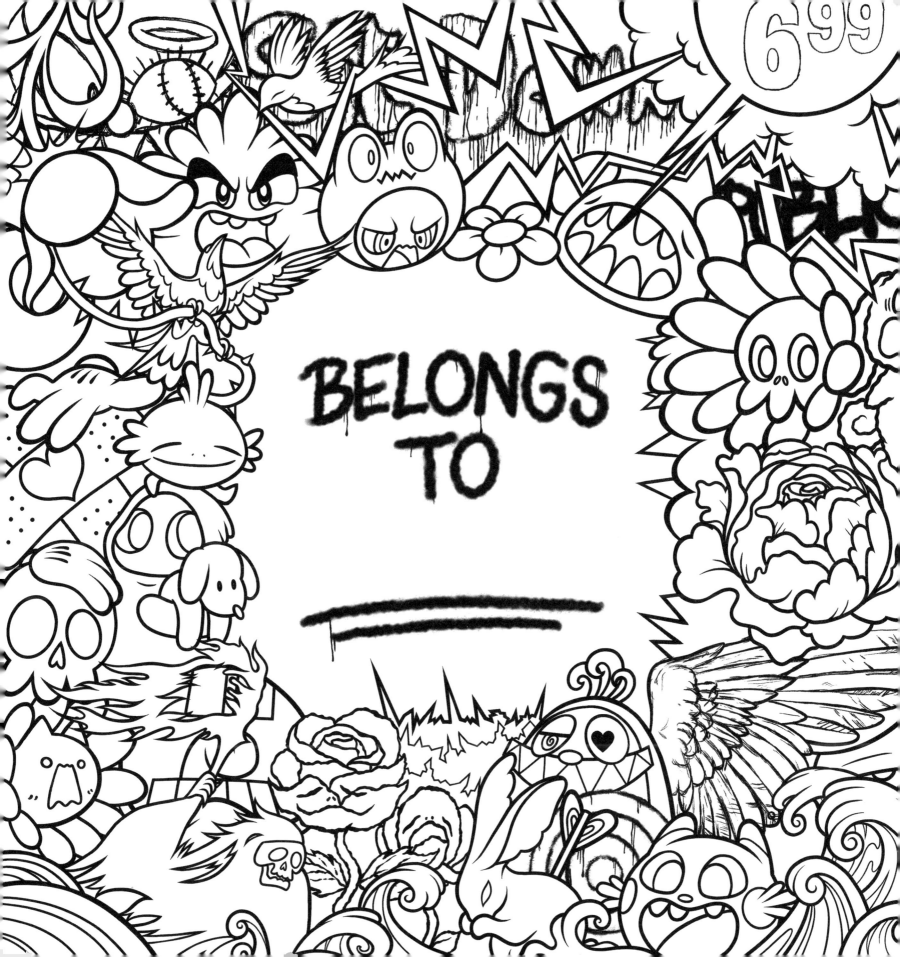

BELONGS
TO
_____

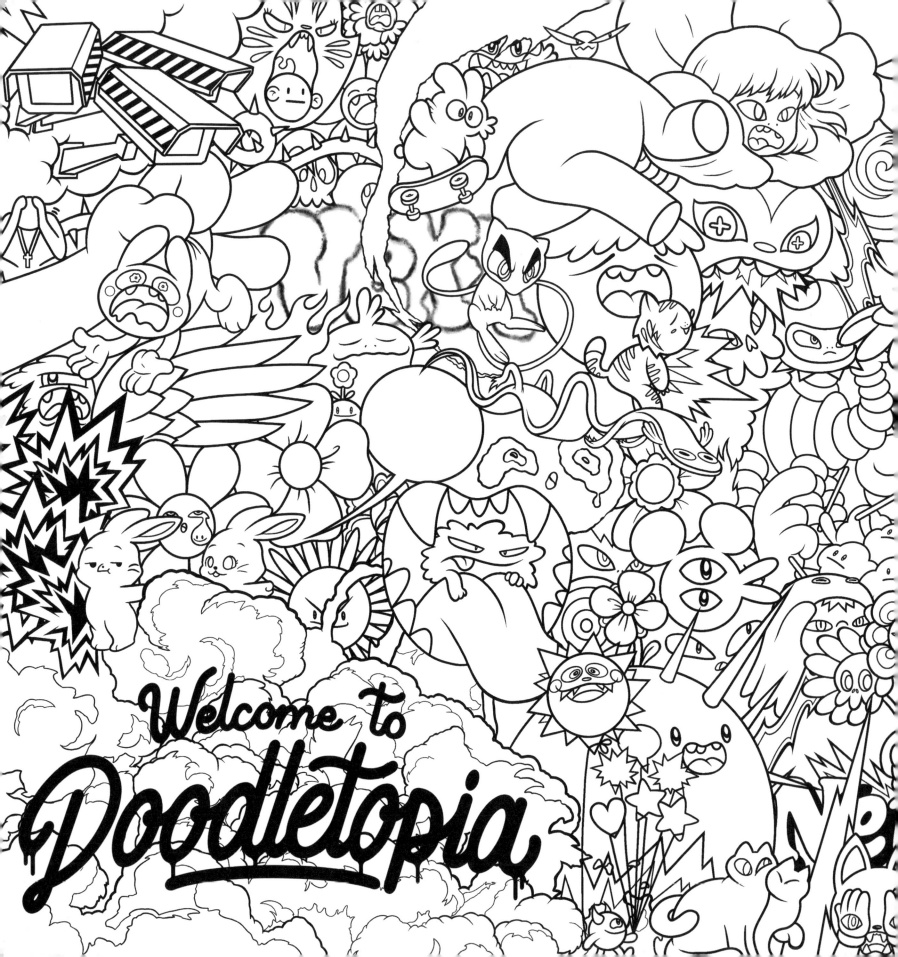

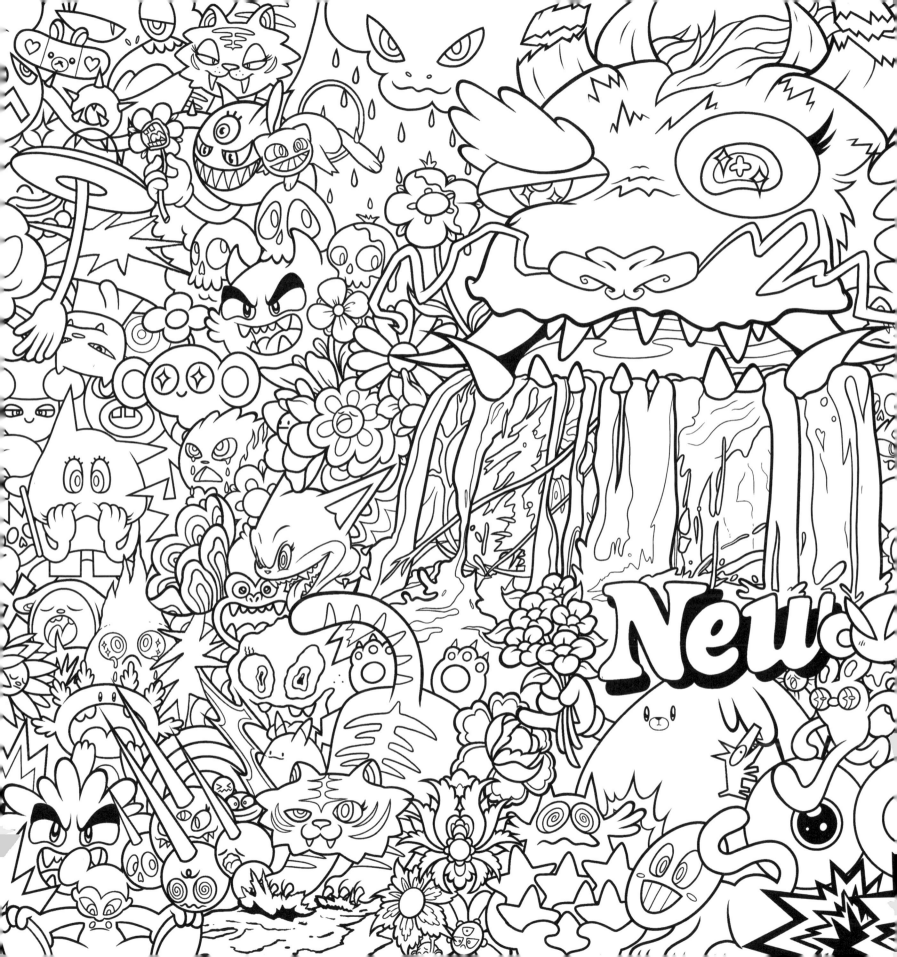

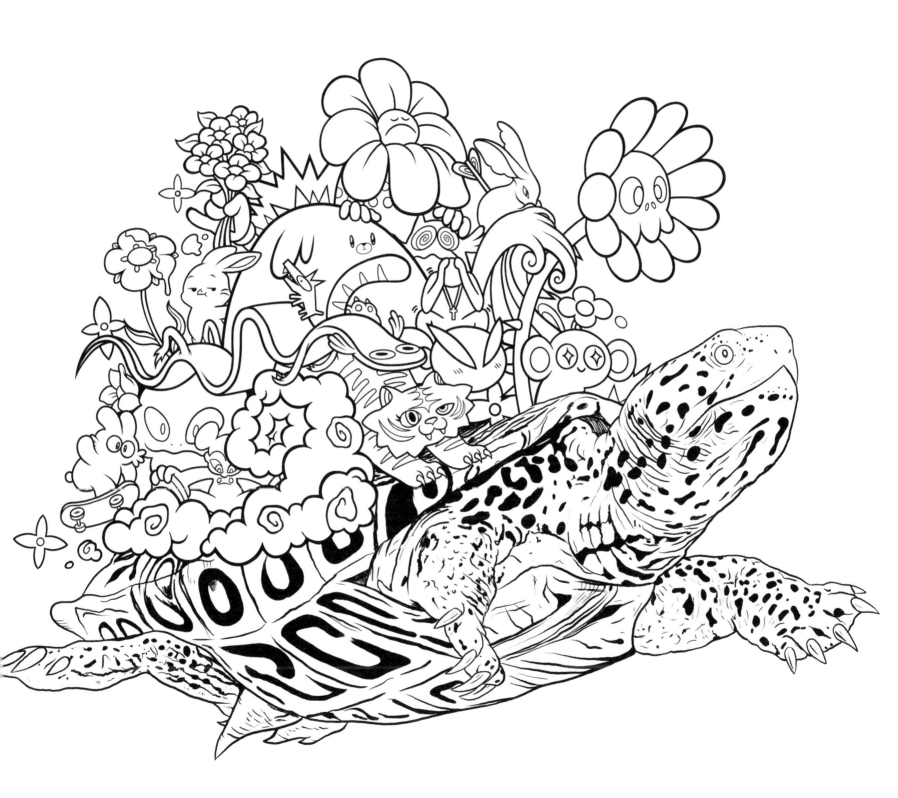

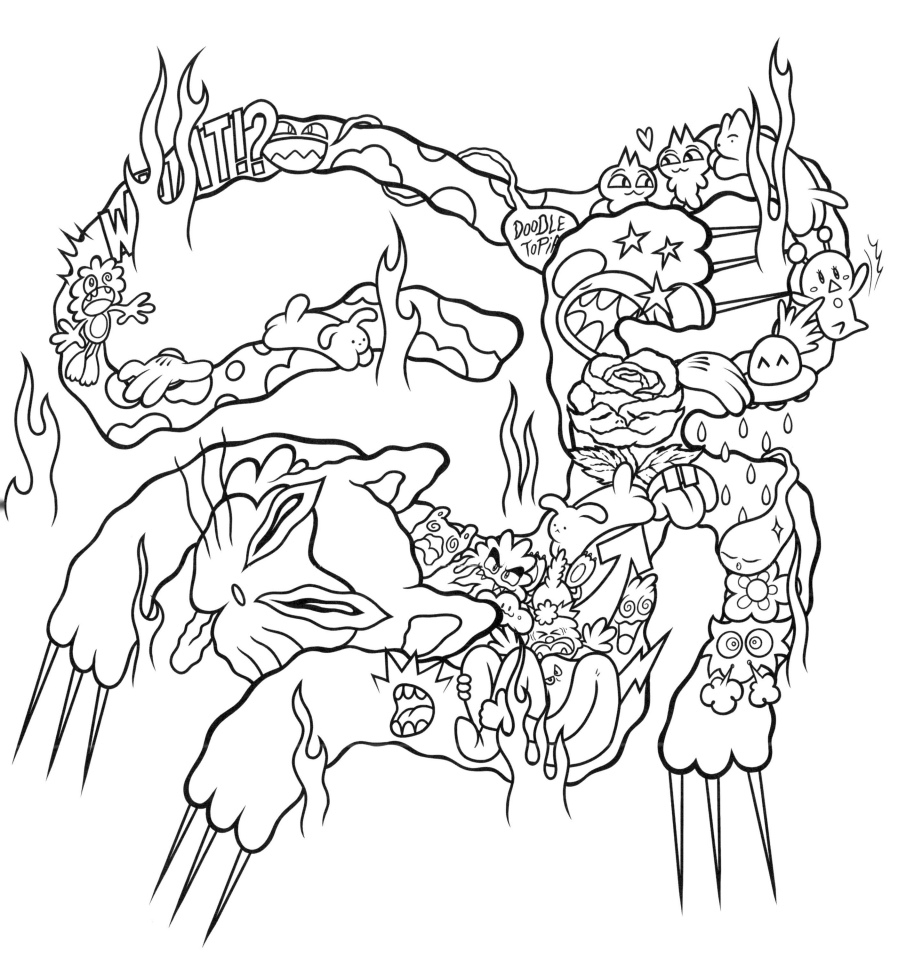

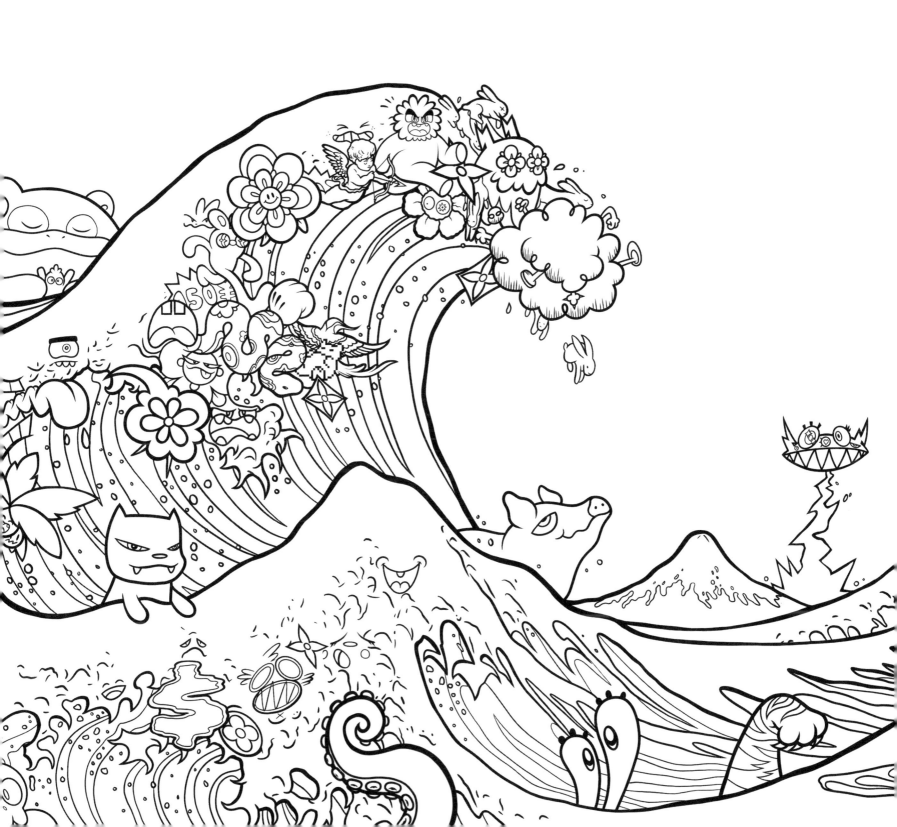

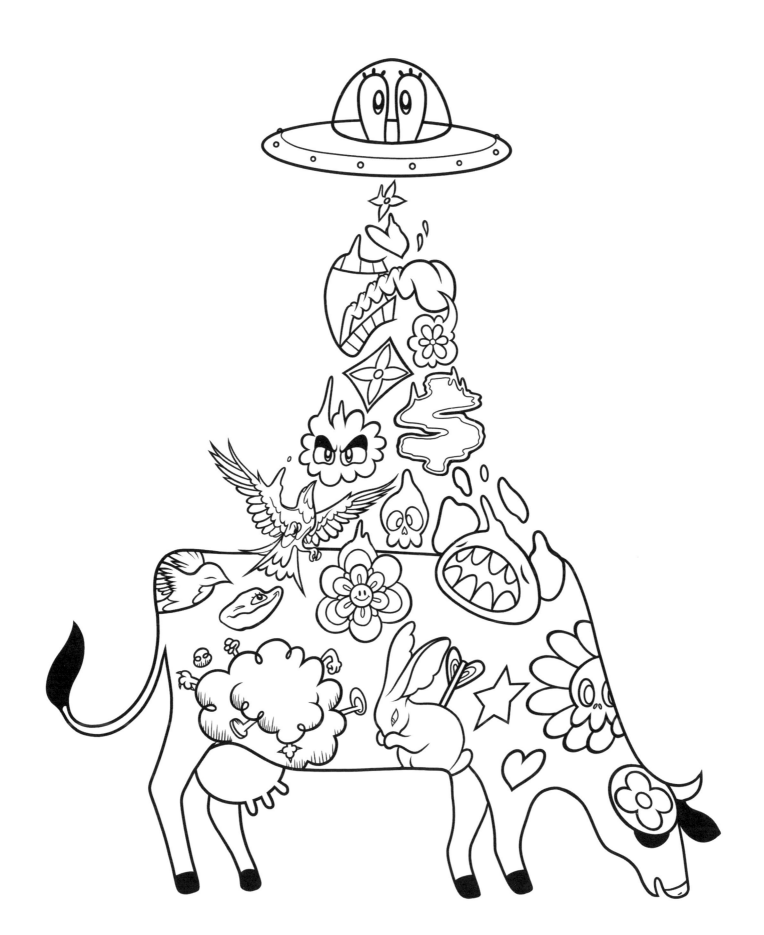

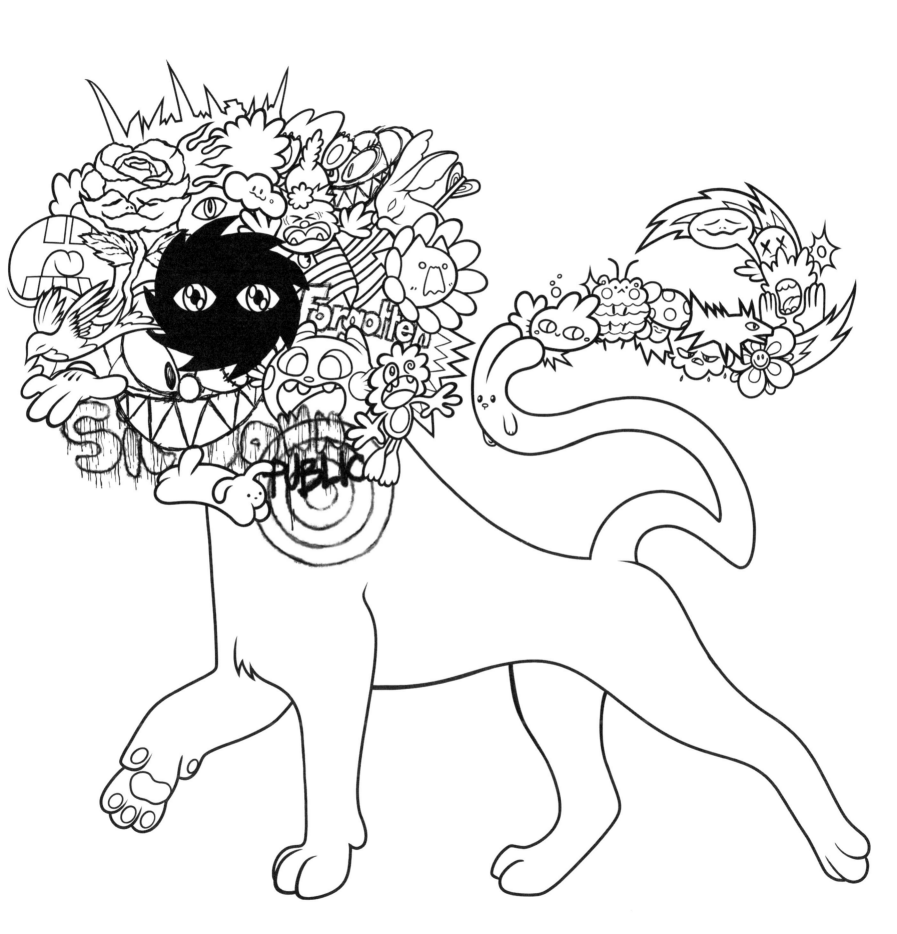

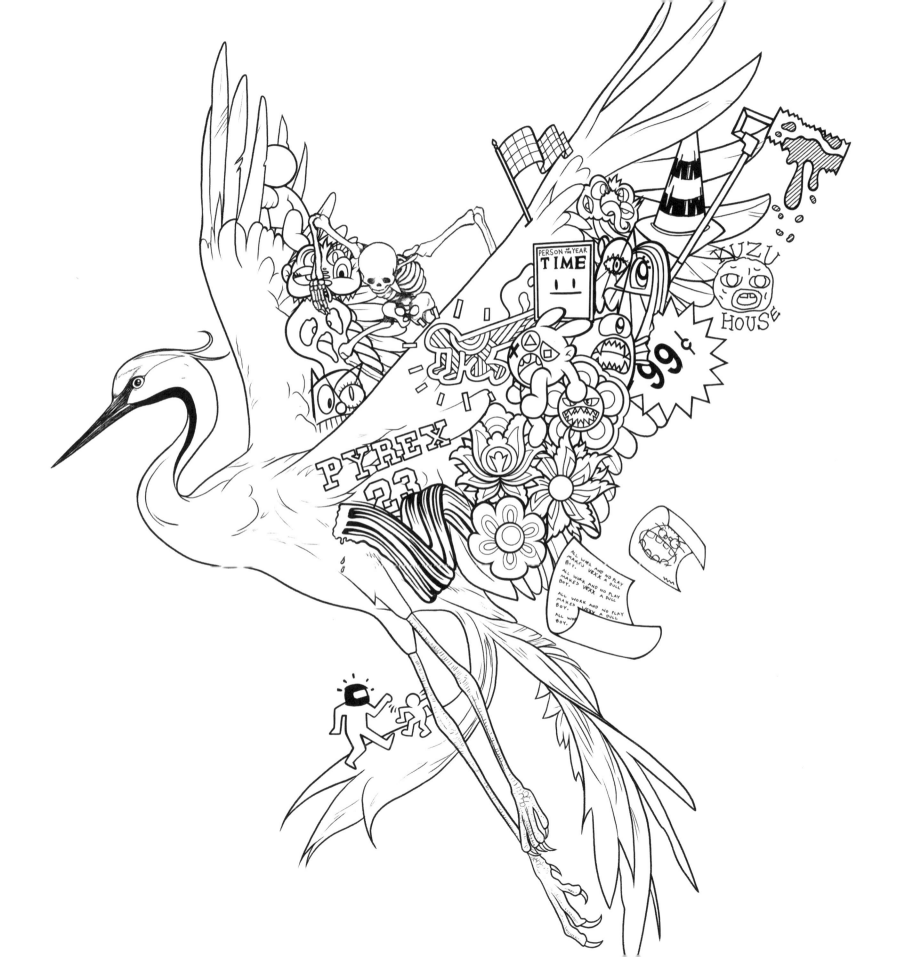

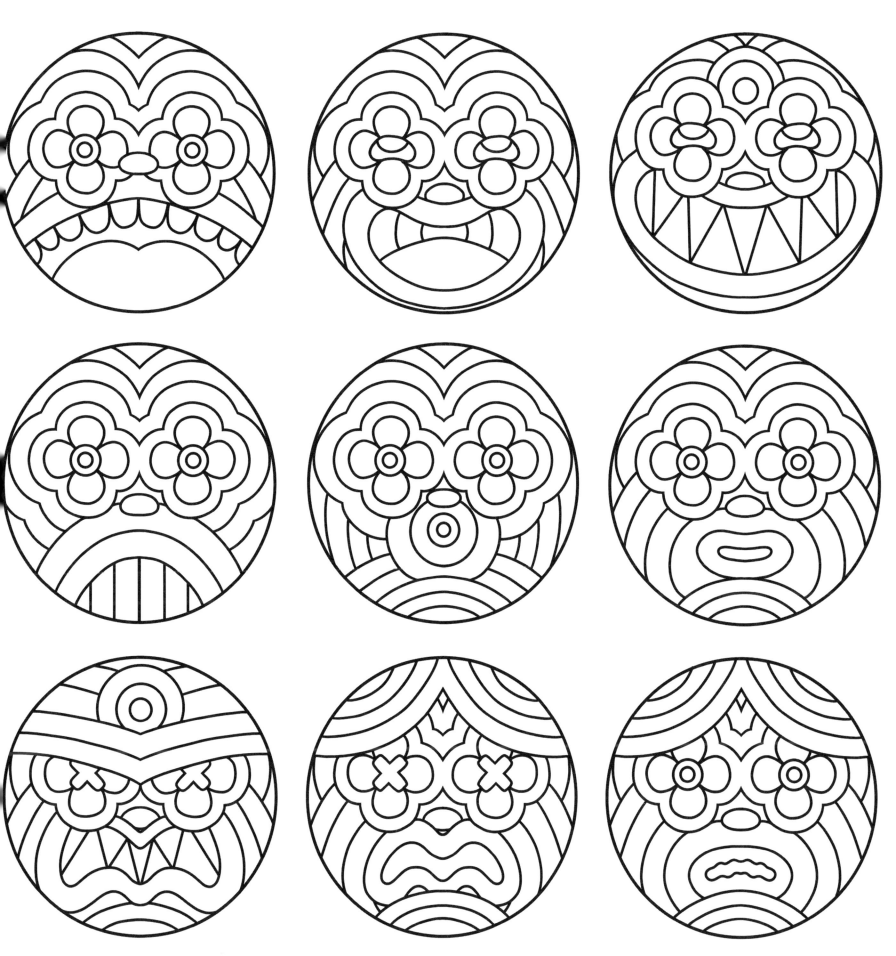

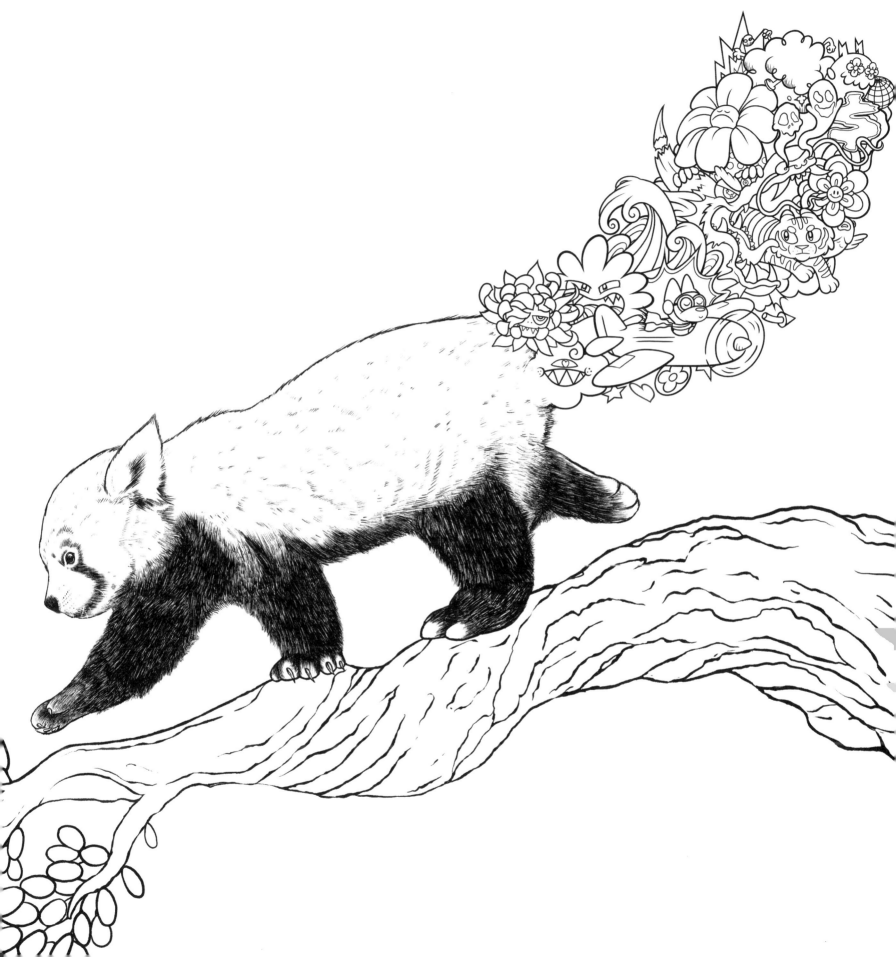

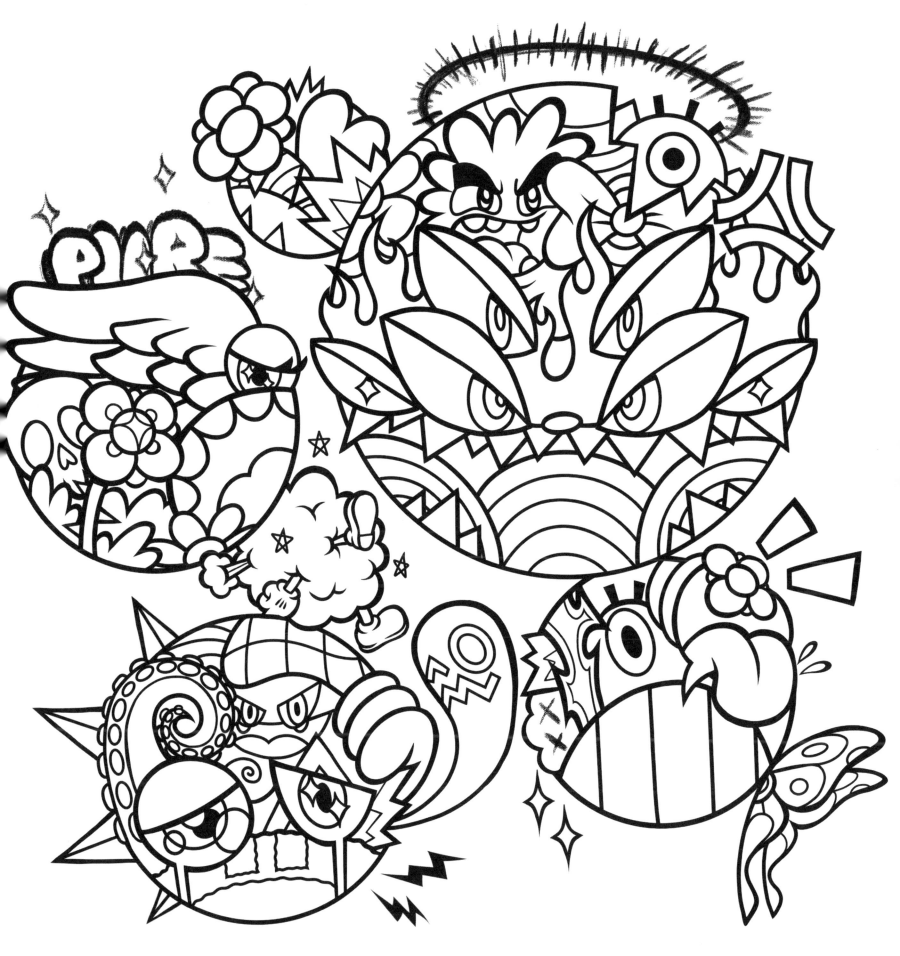

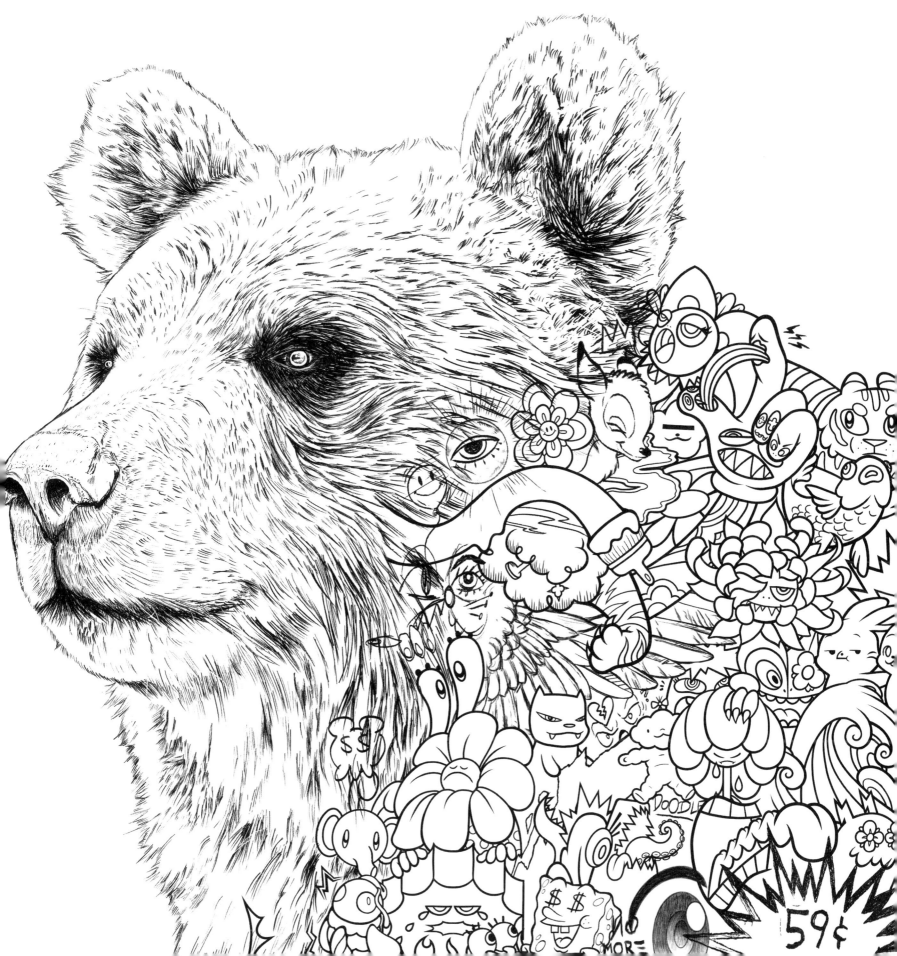

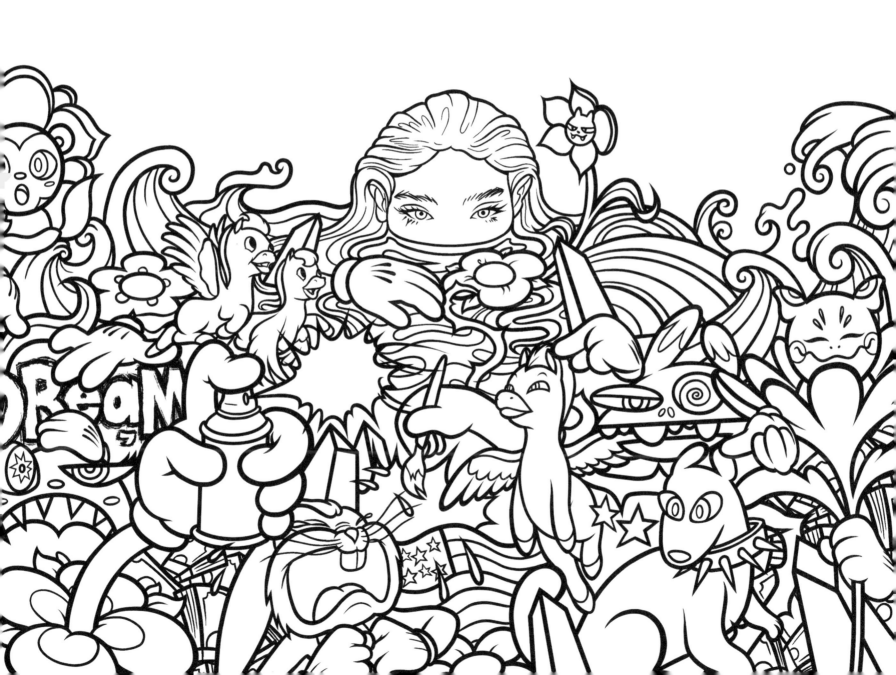

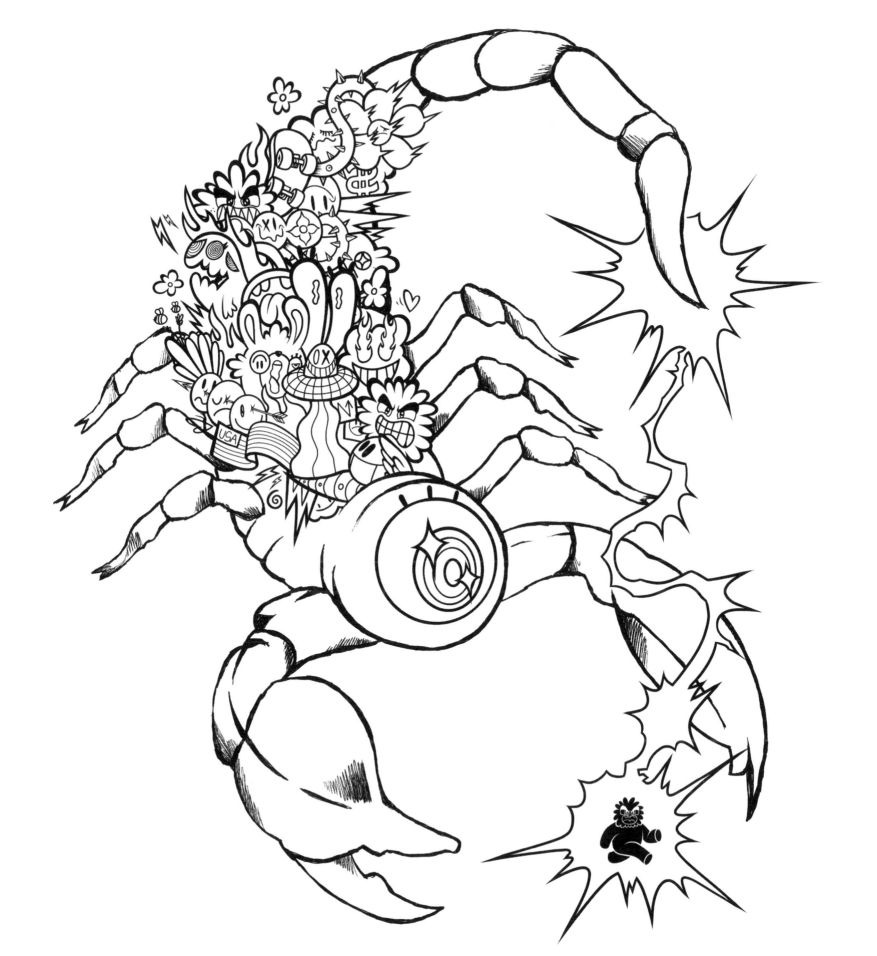

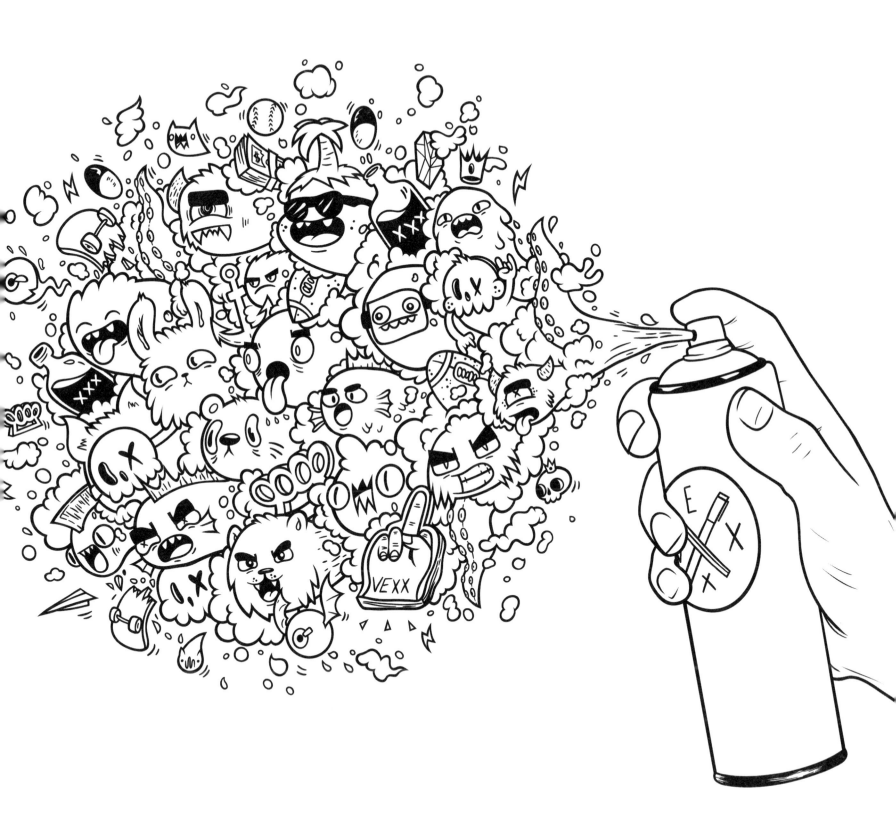

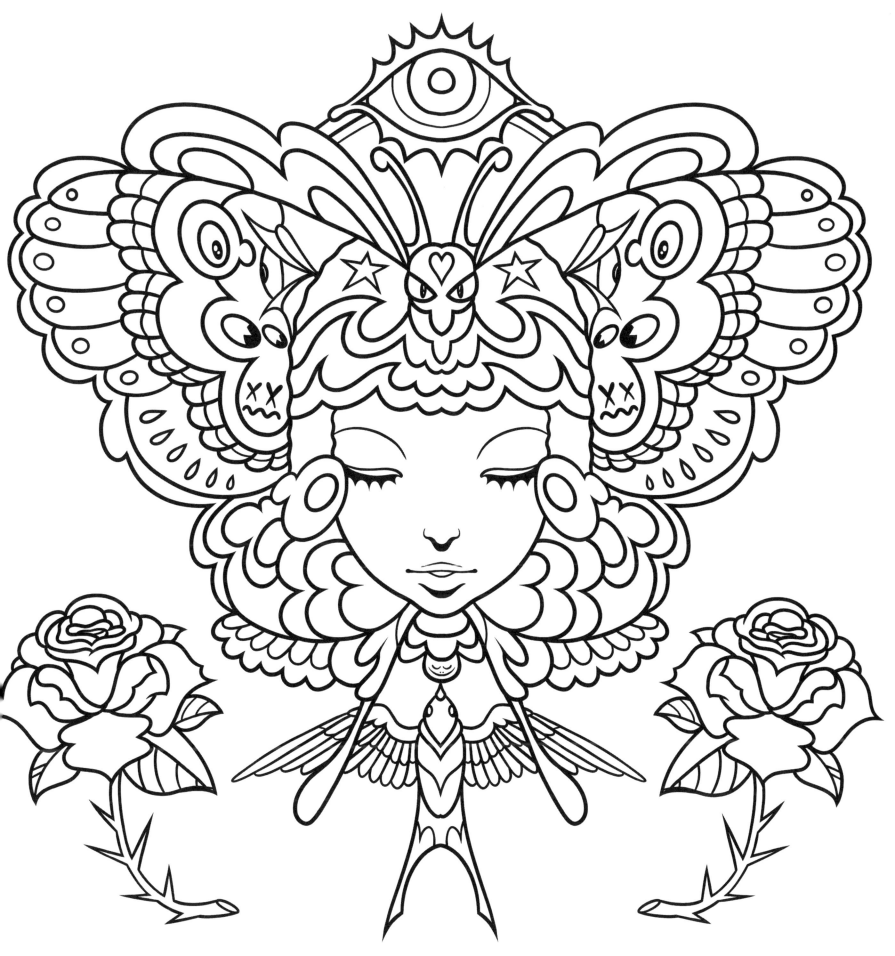

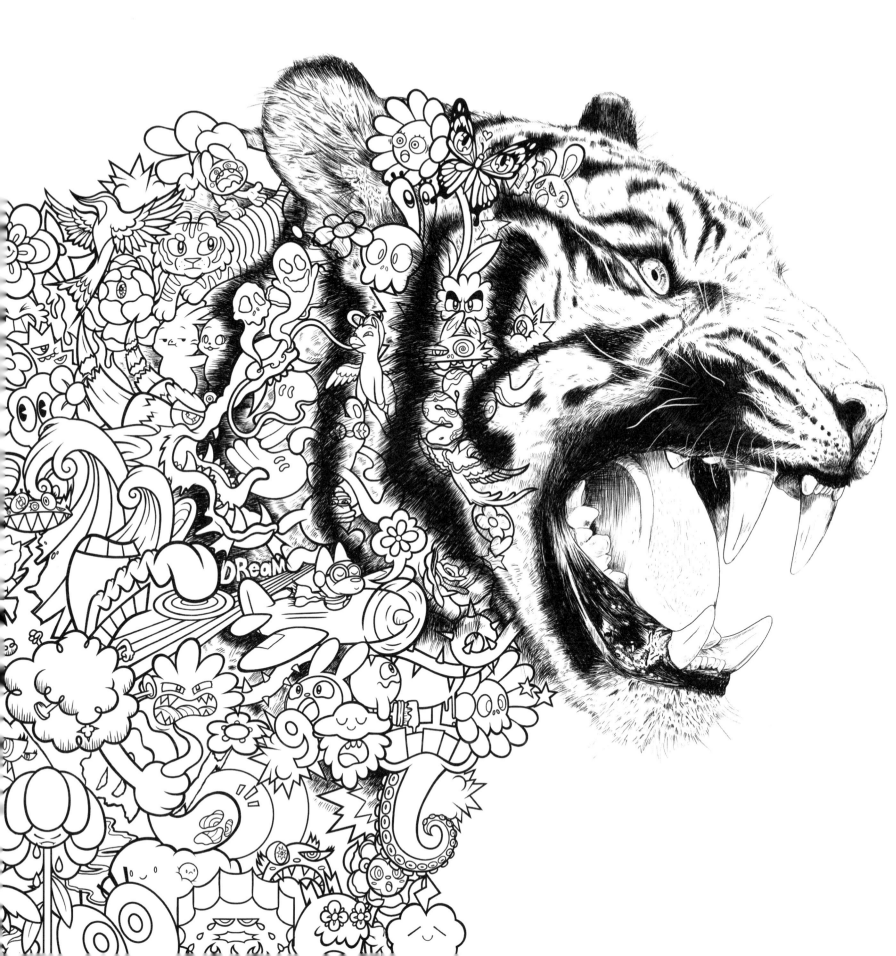

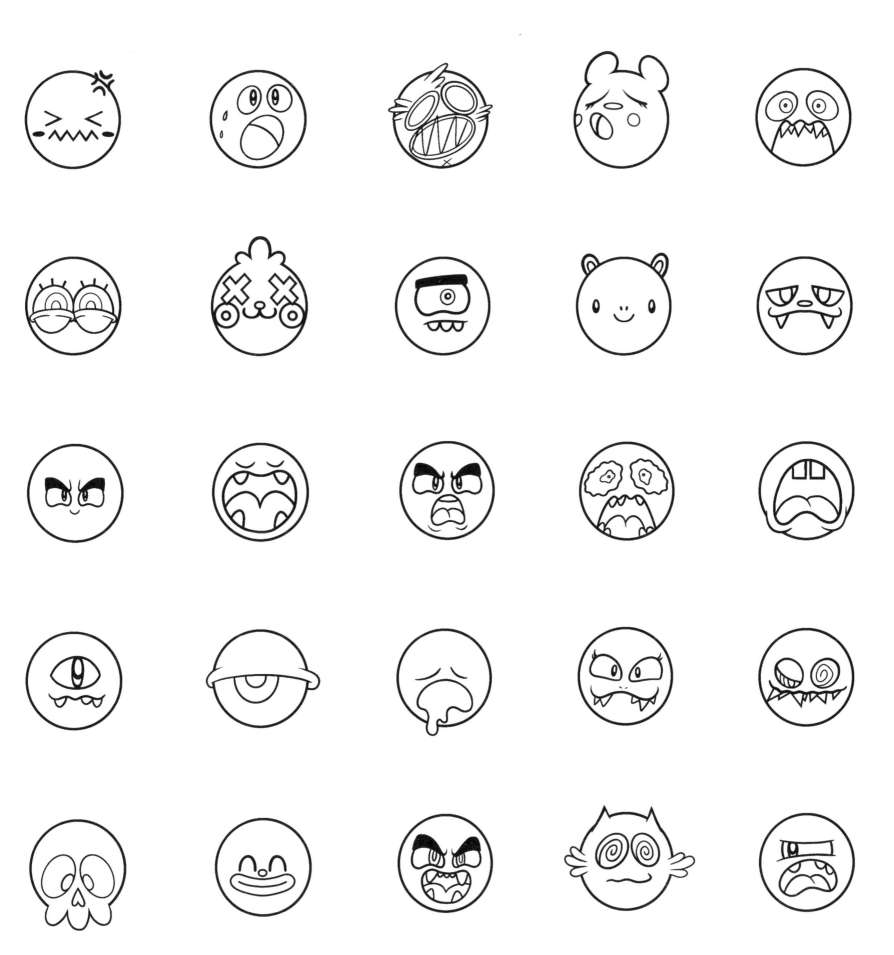

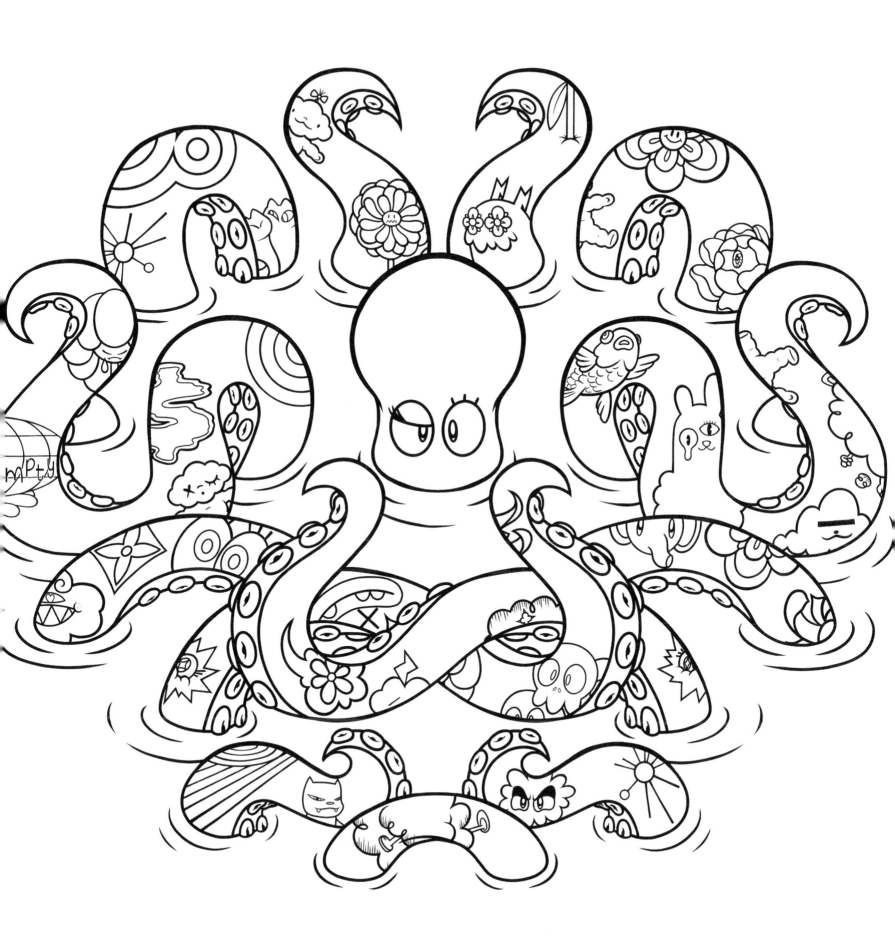

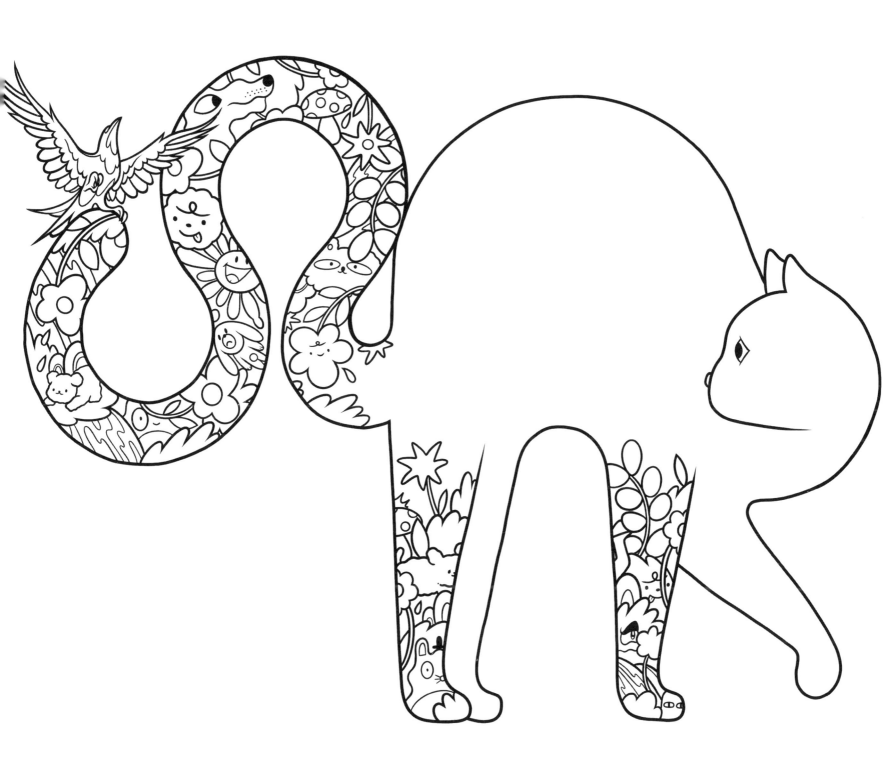

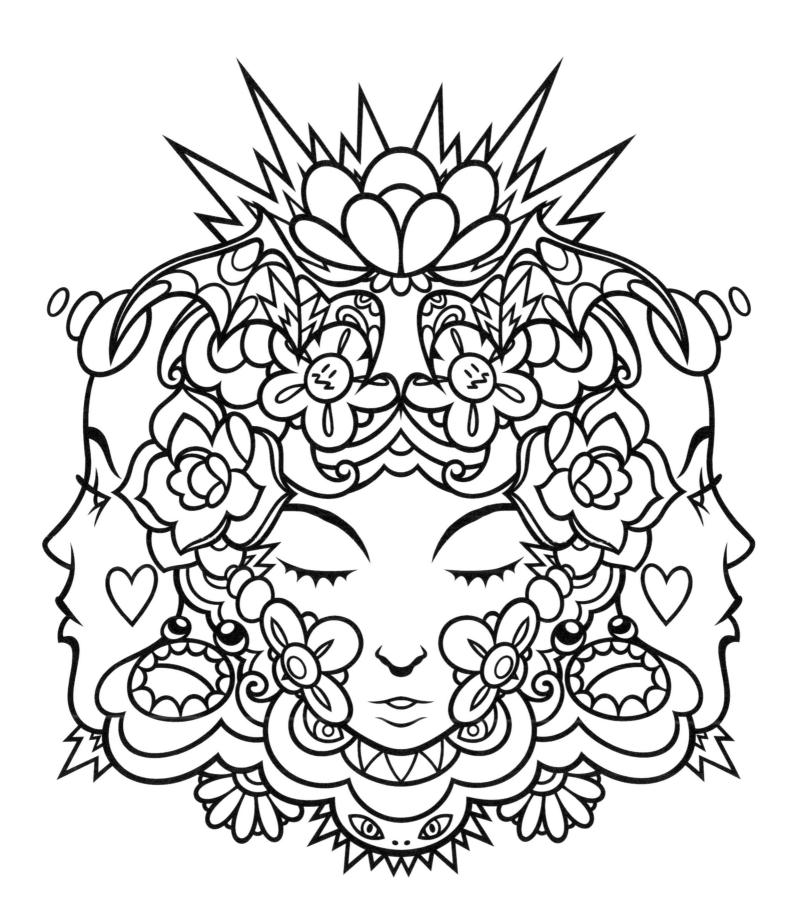

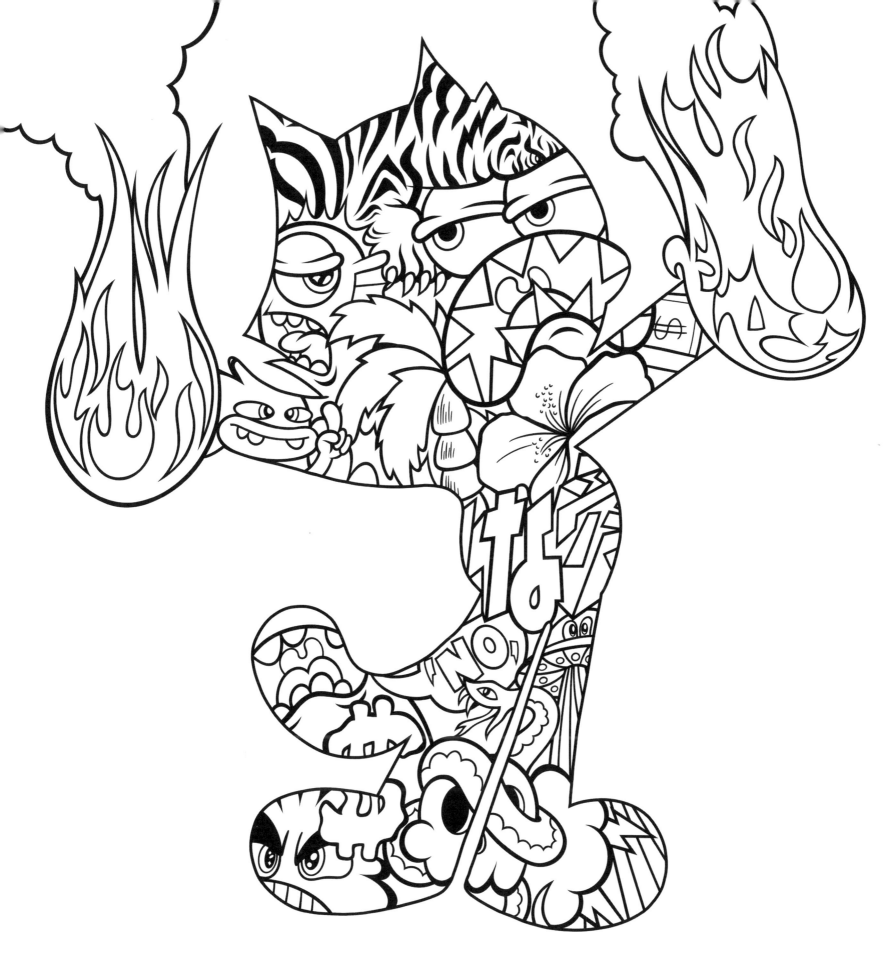

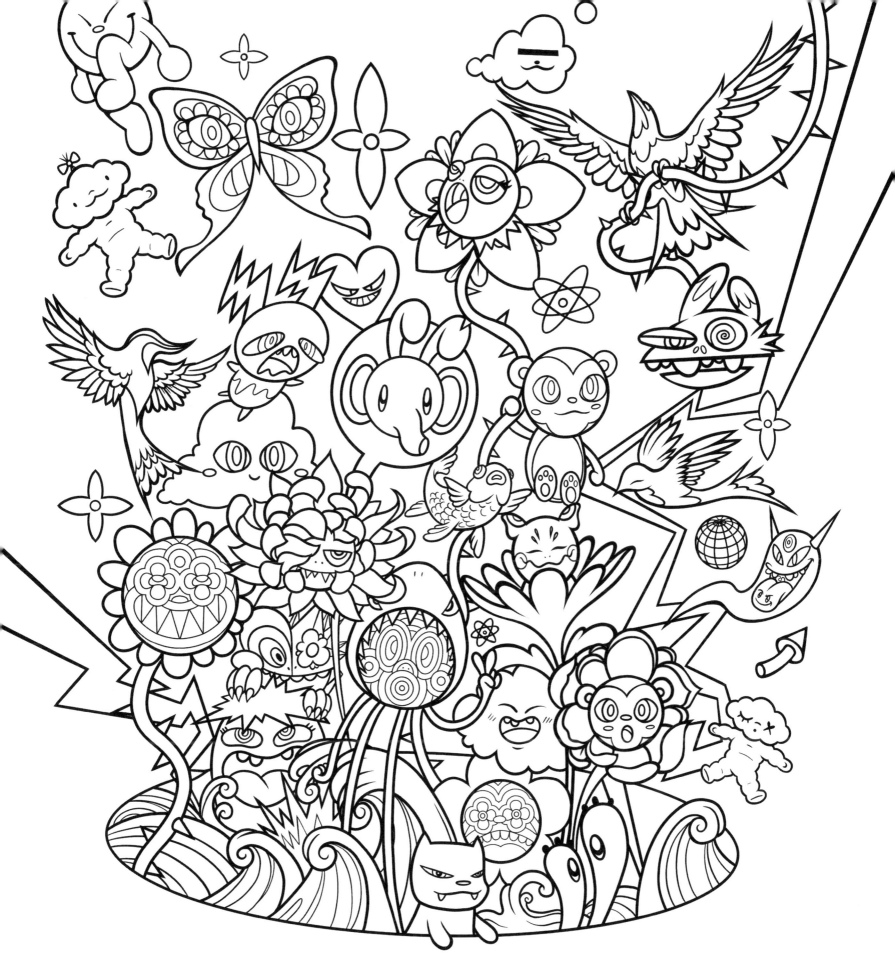

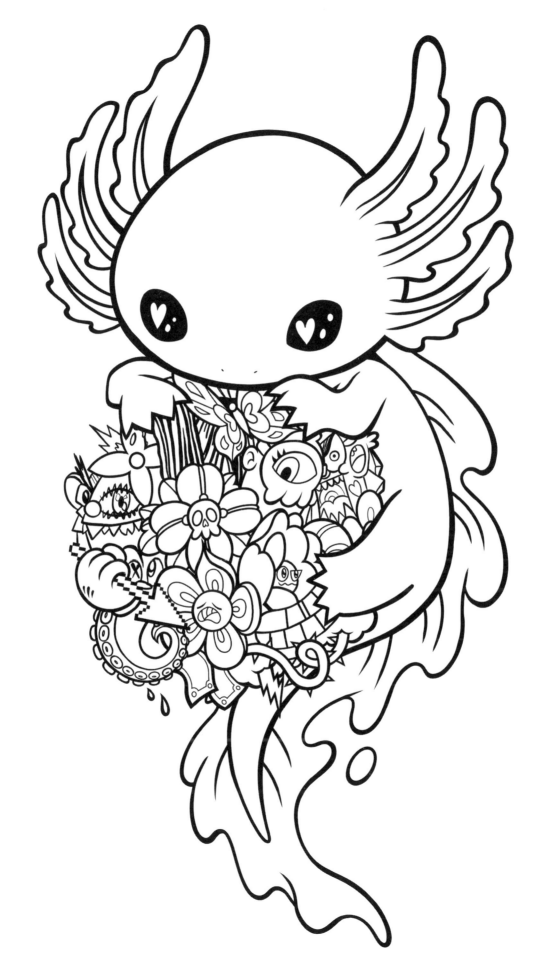

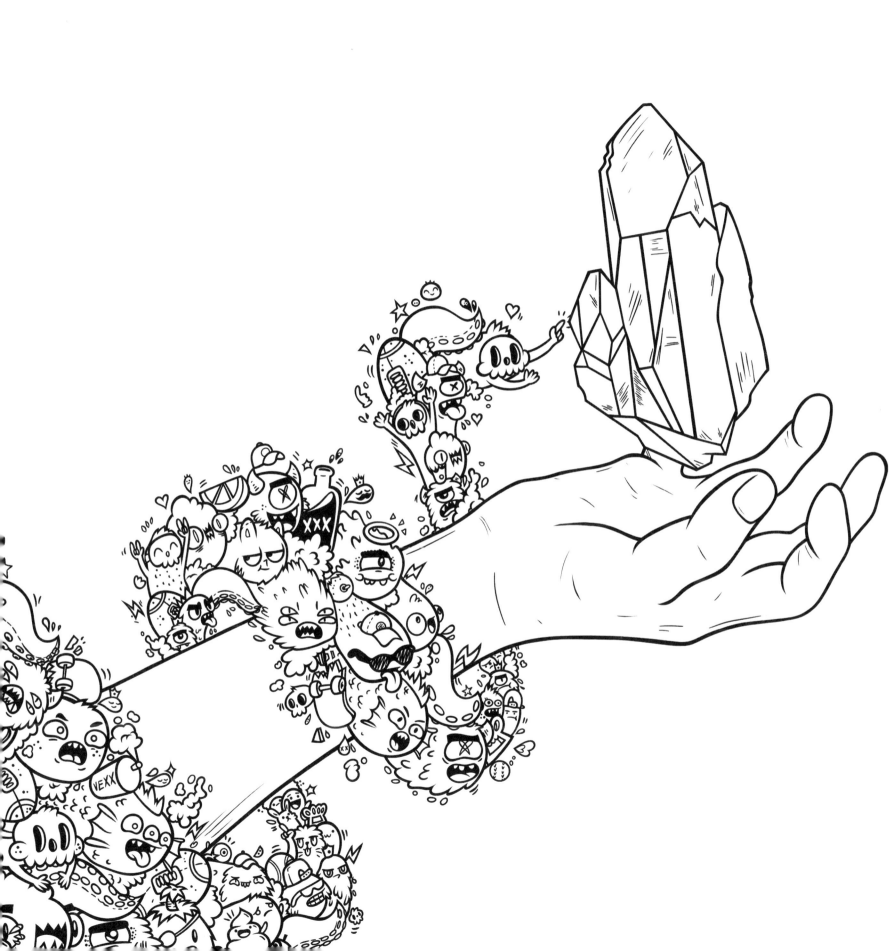

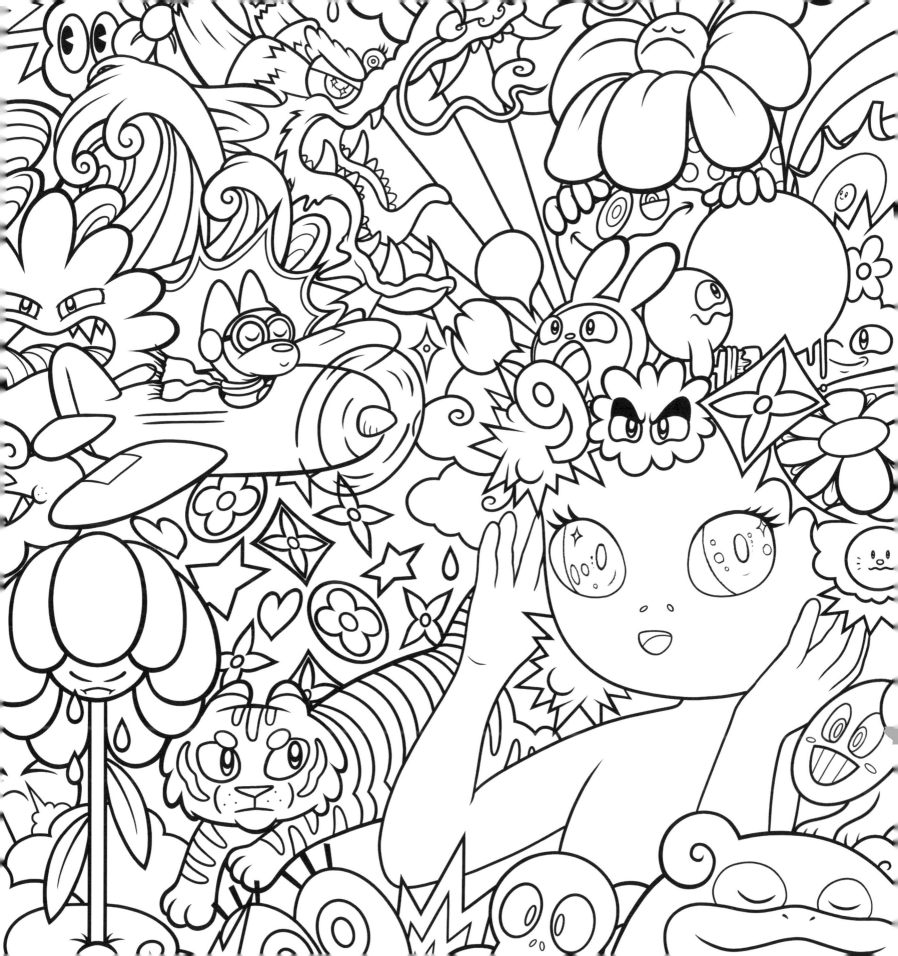

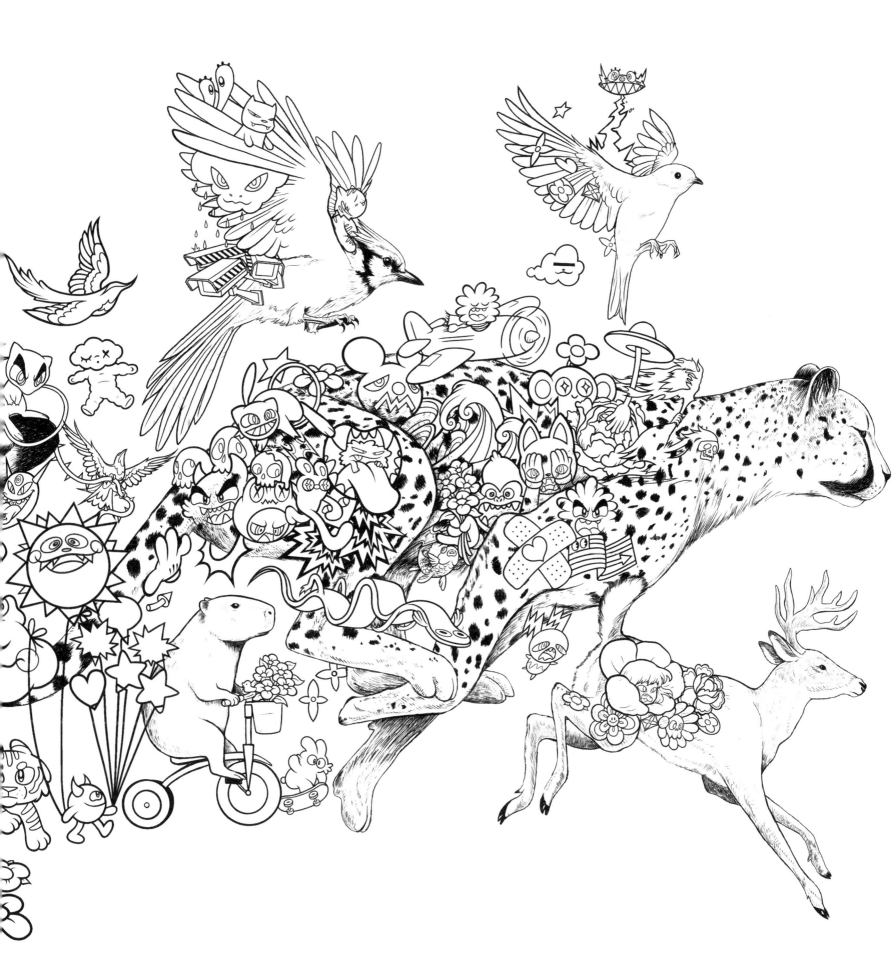

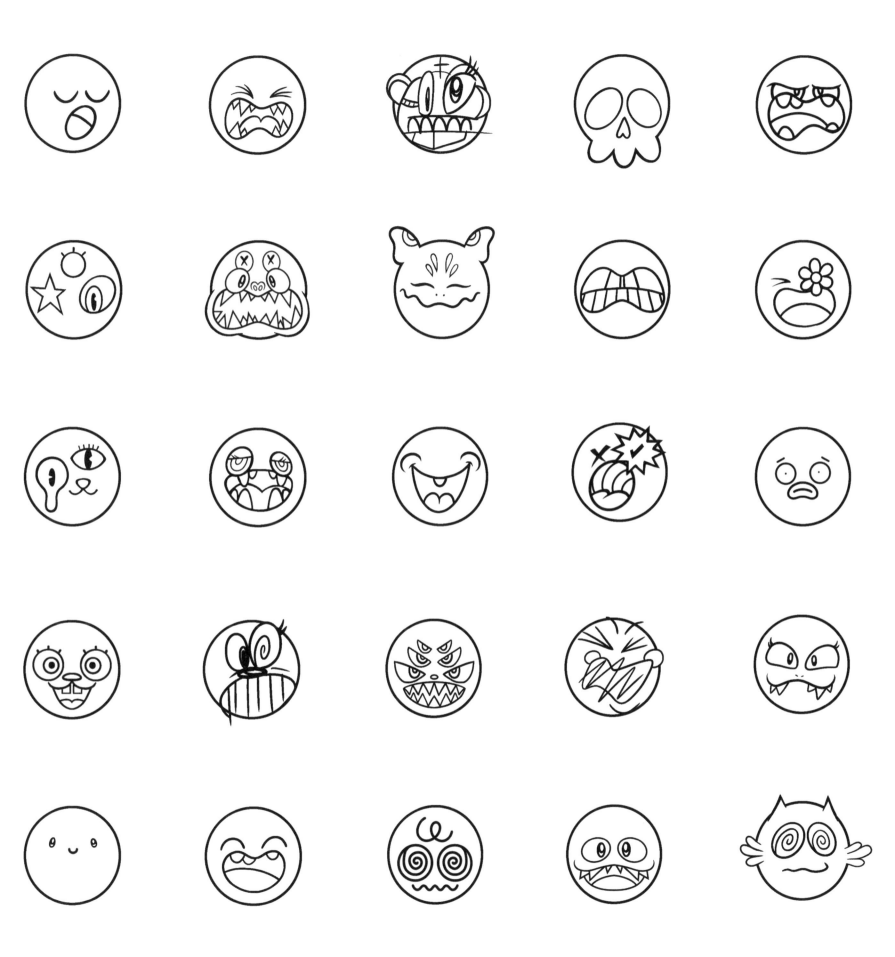

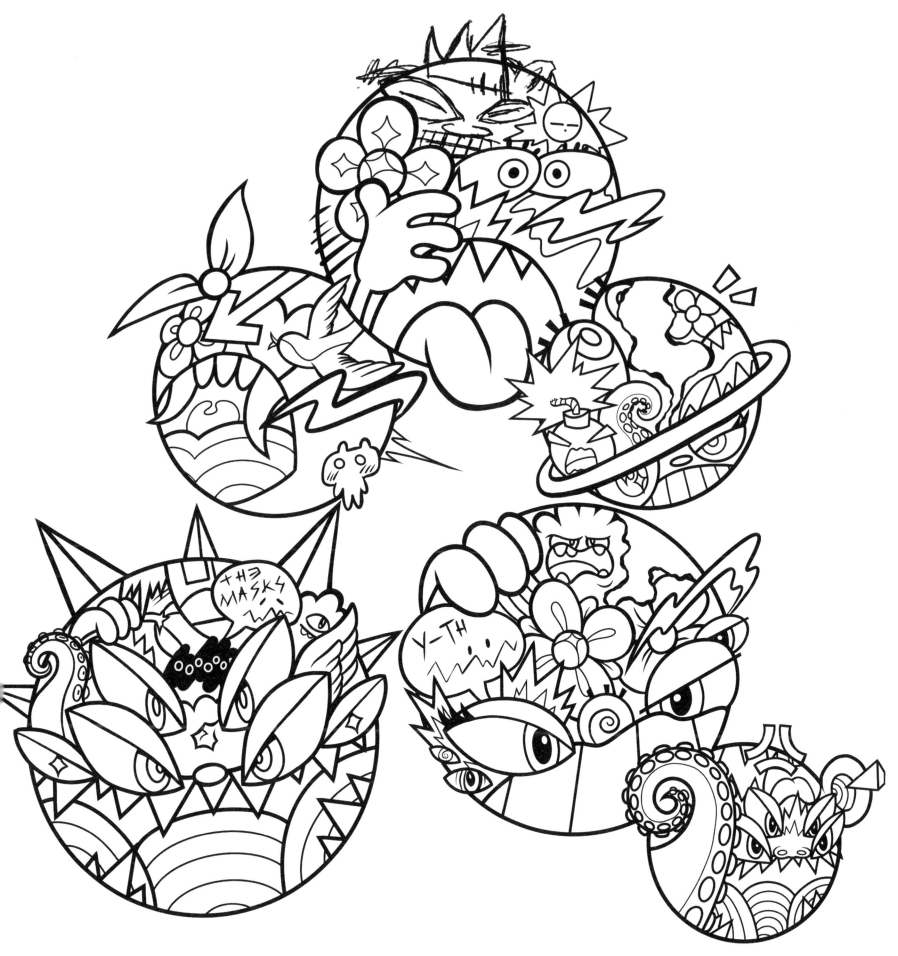

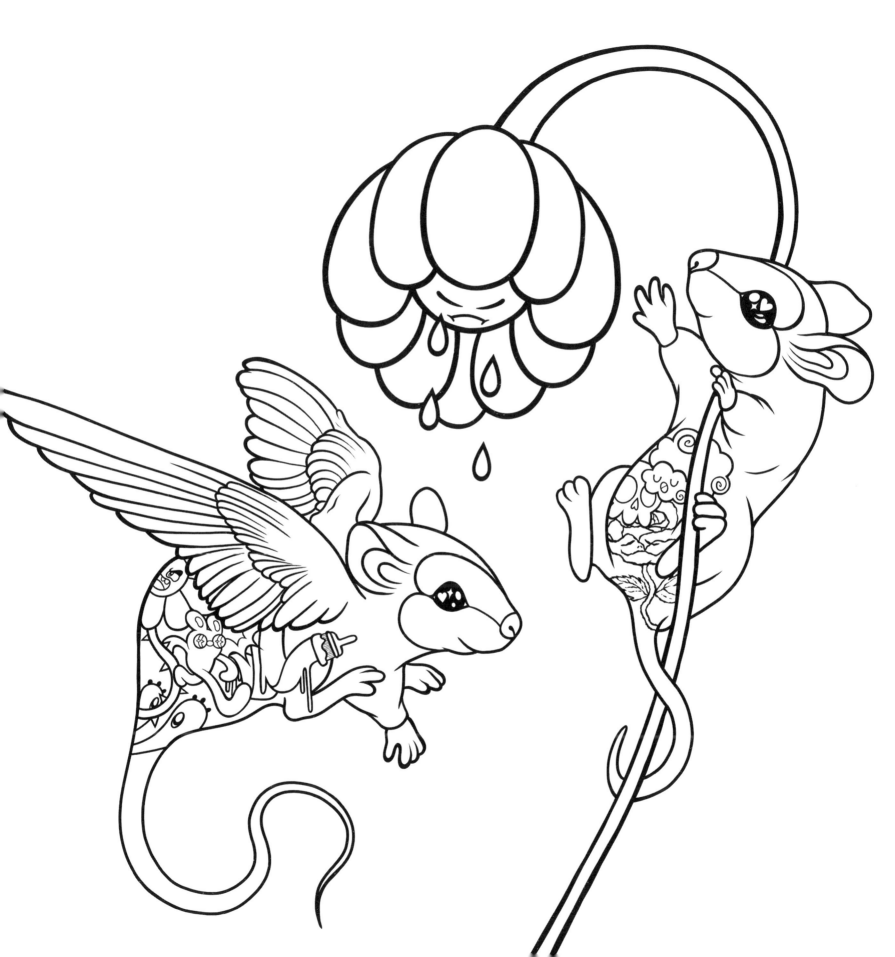

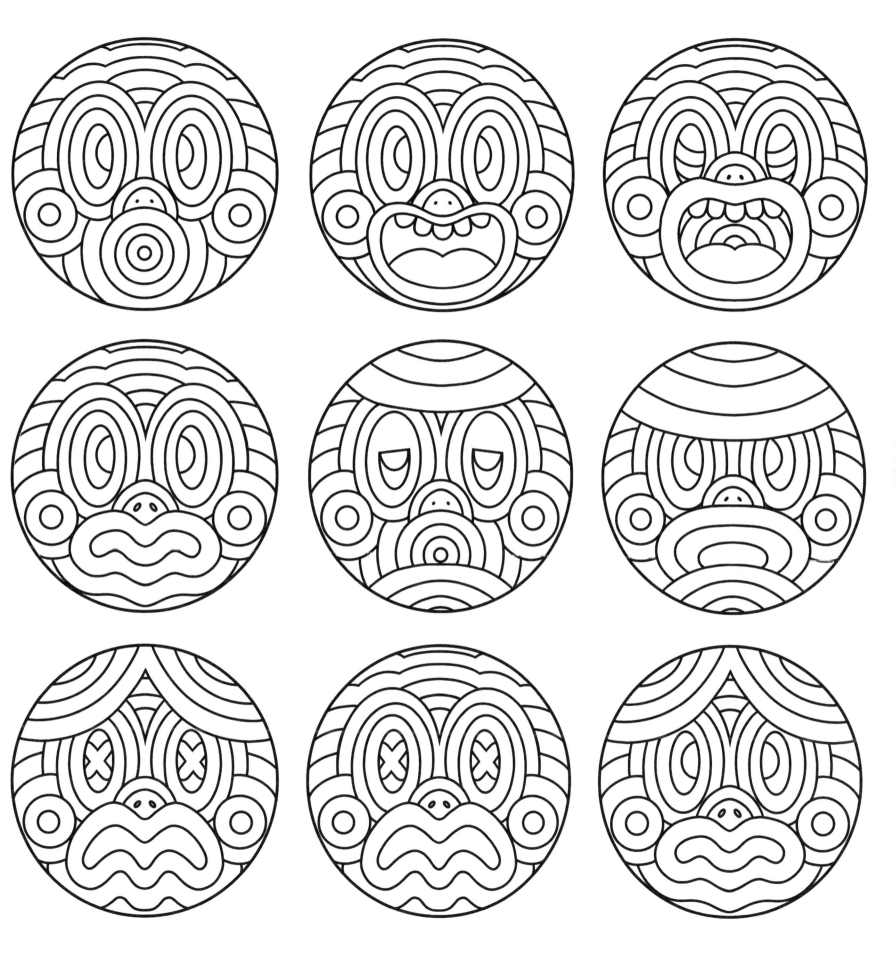

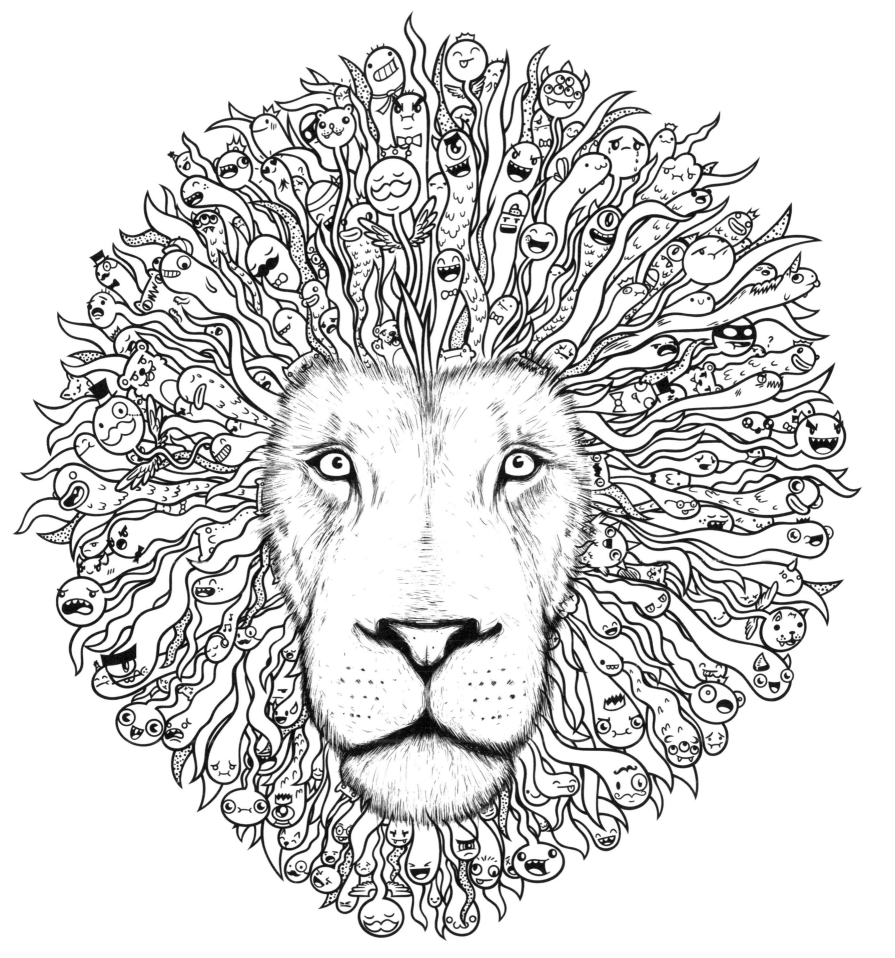

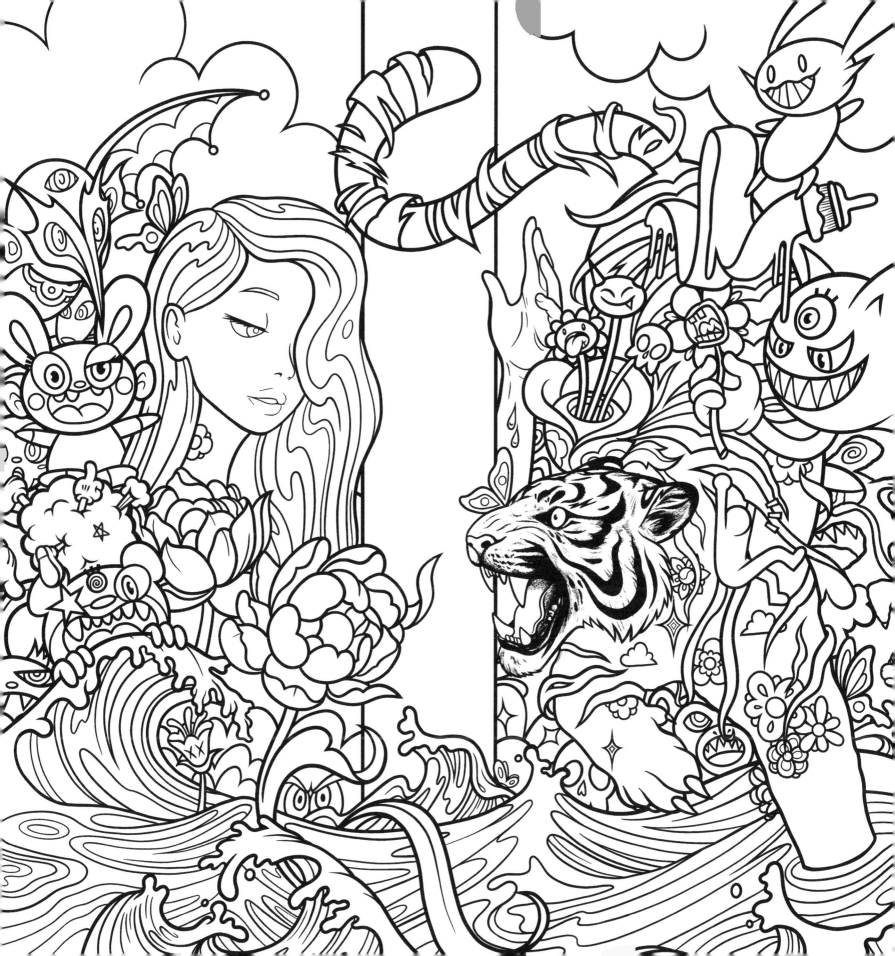

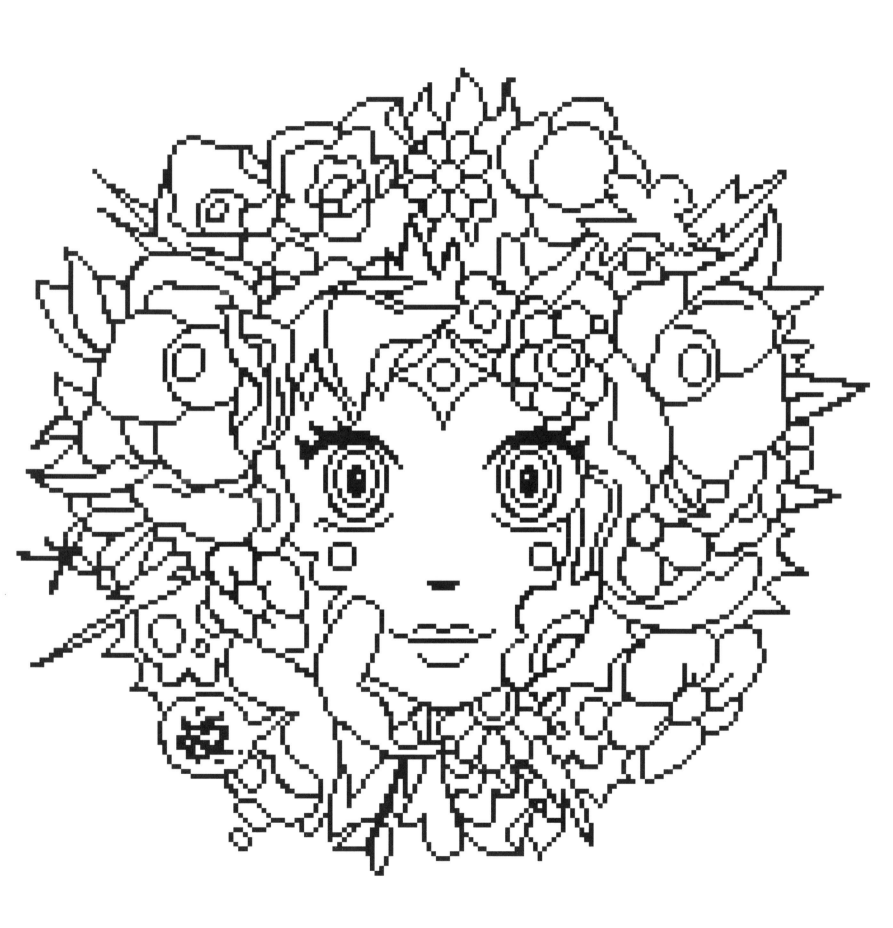

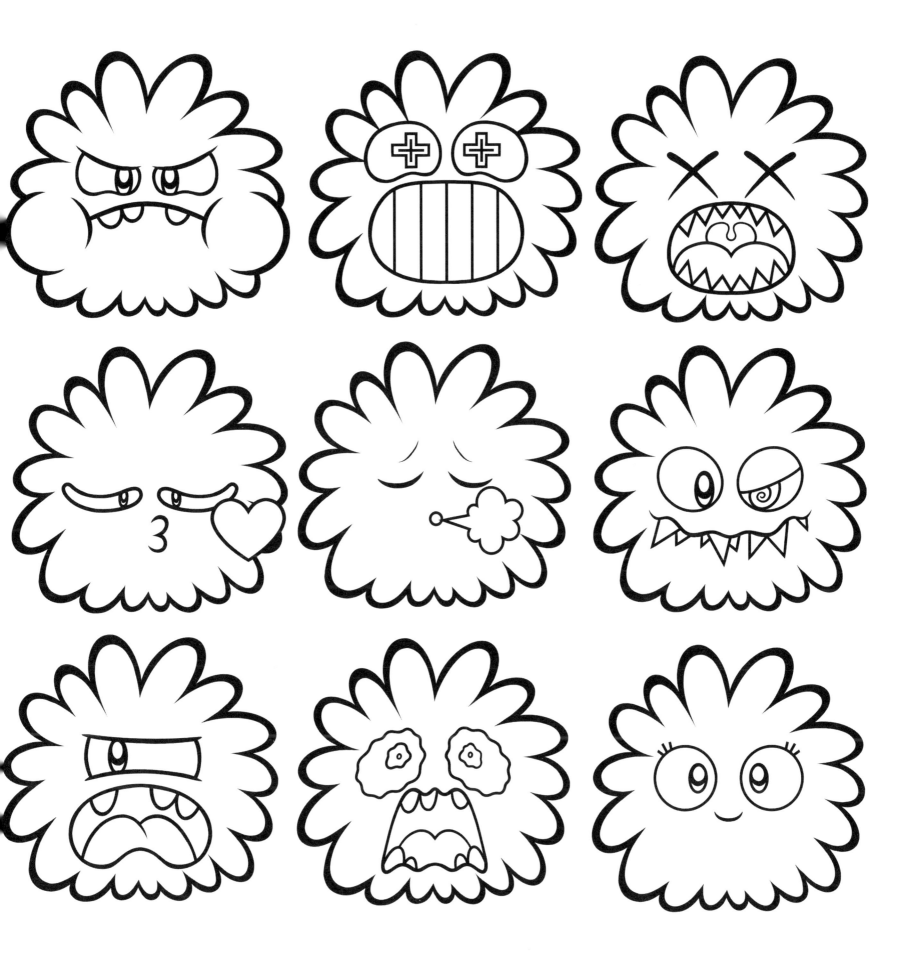

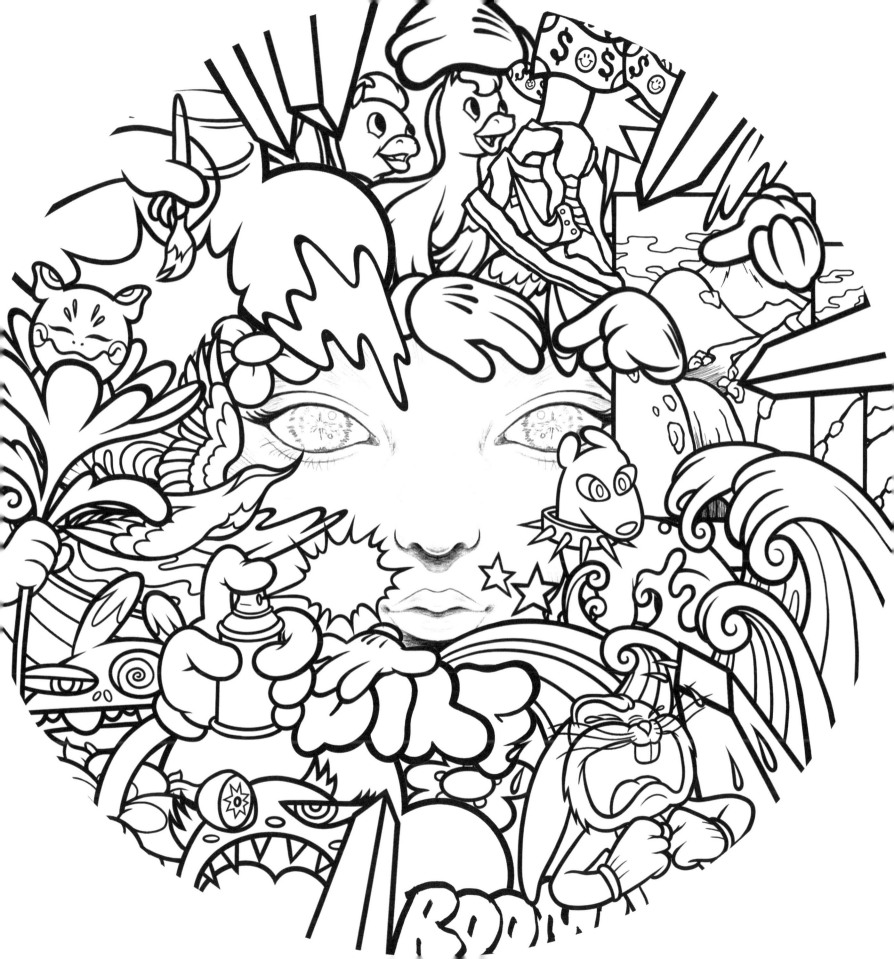

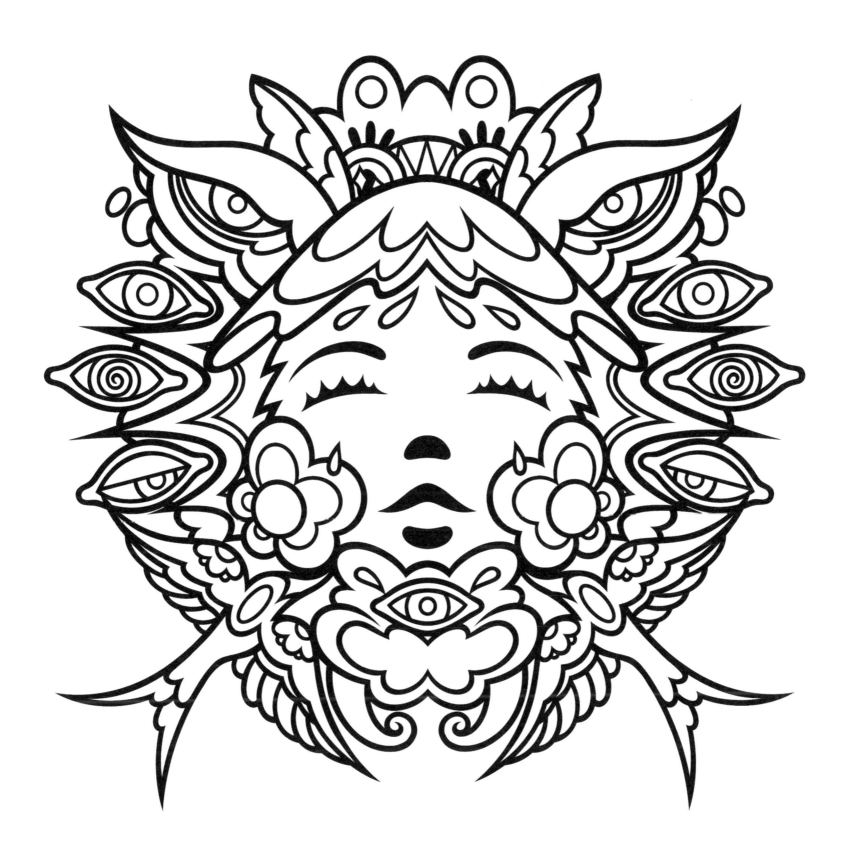

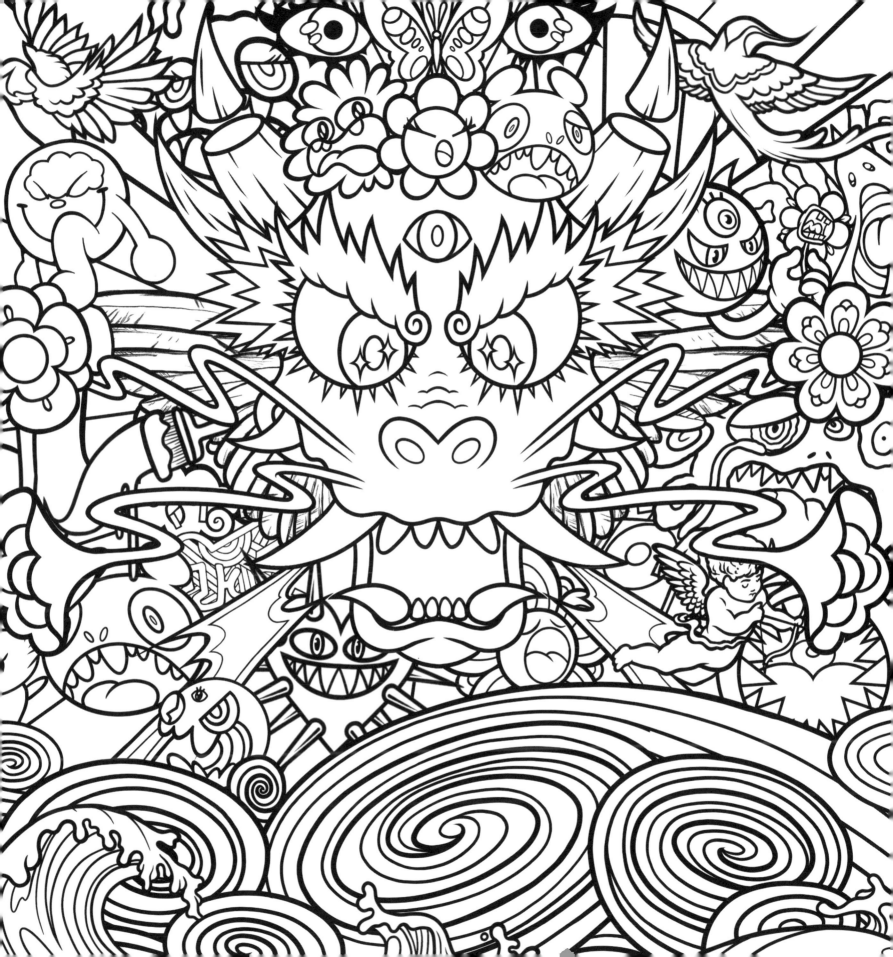

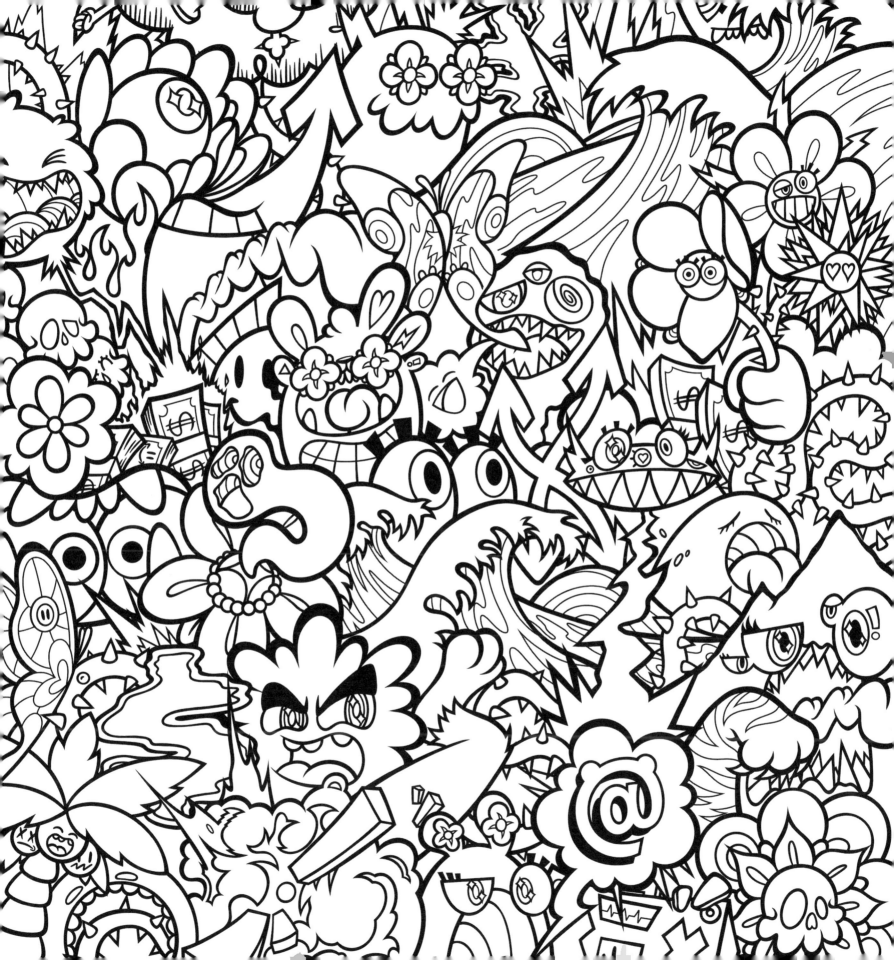

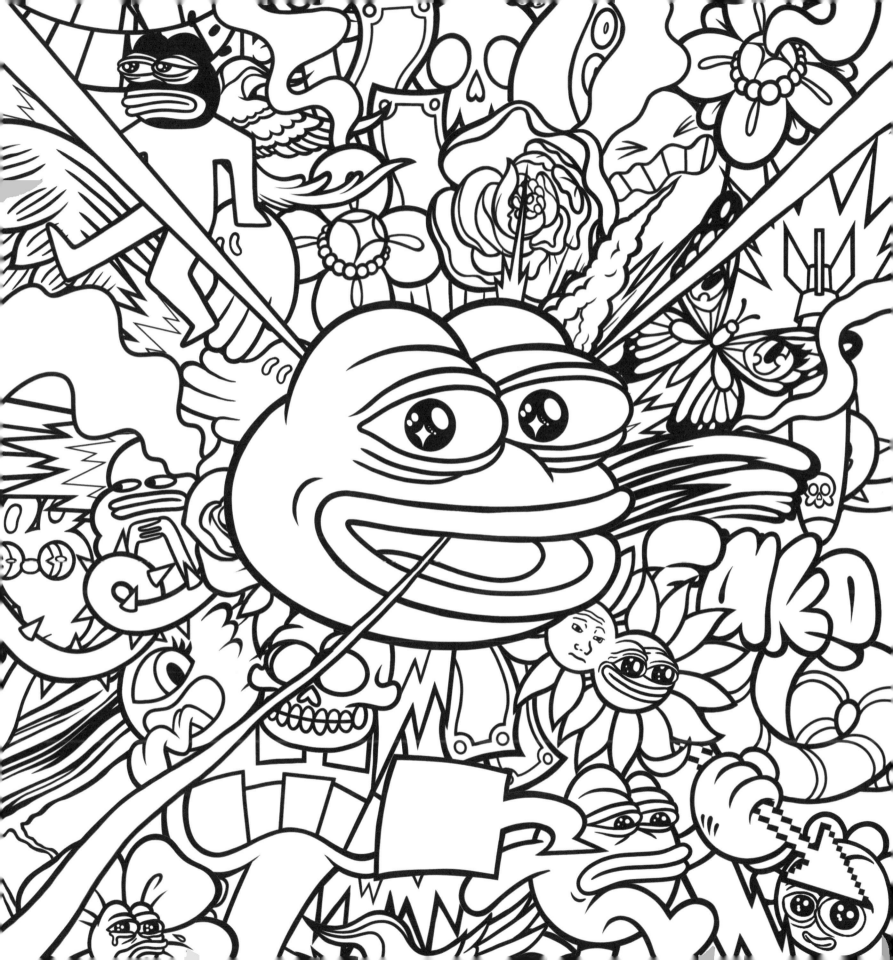

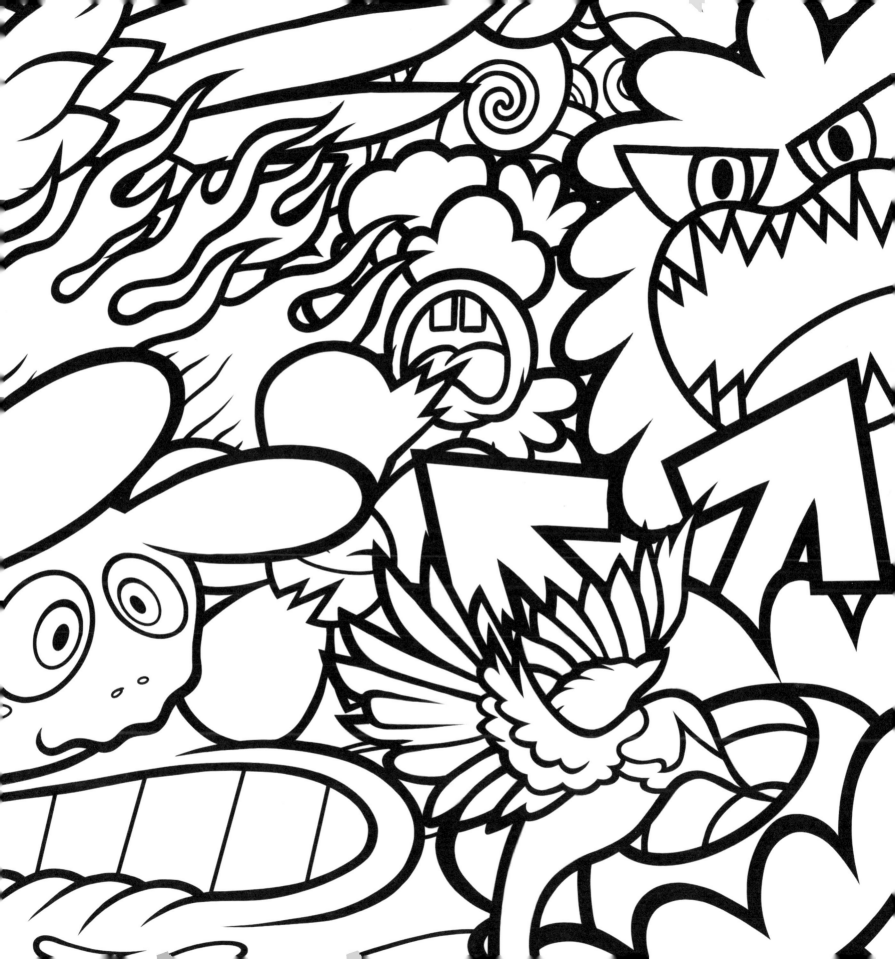

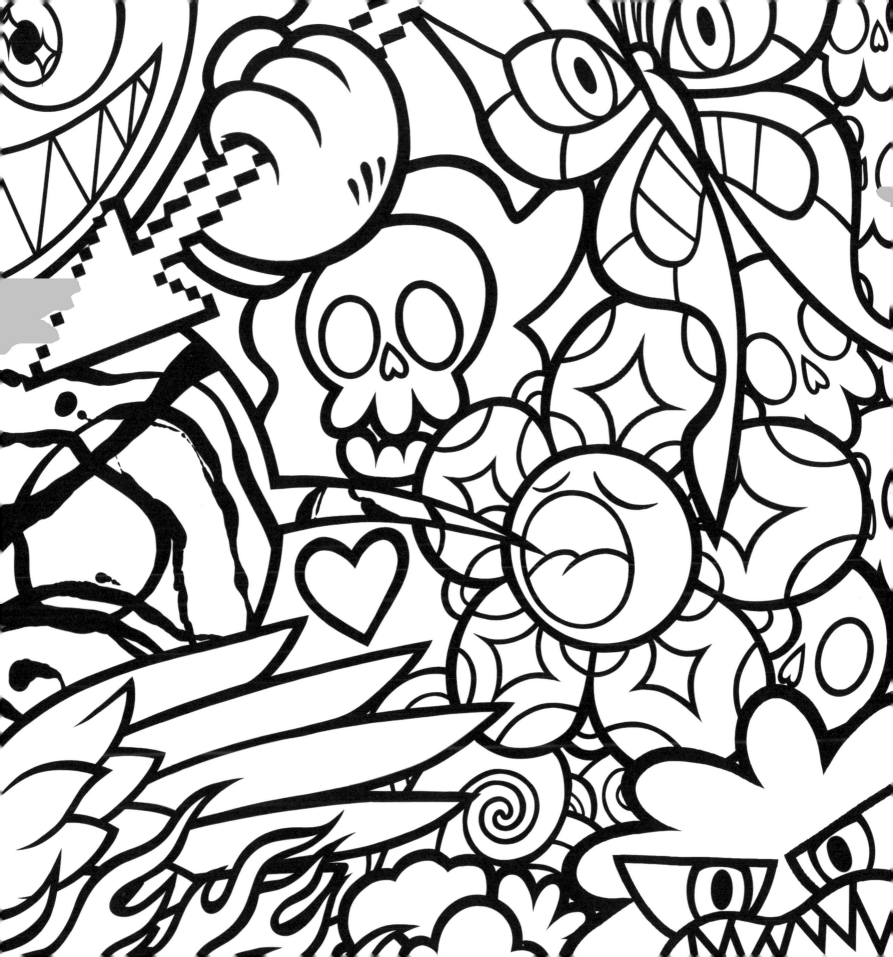

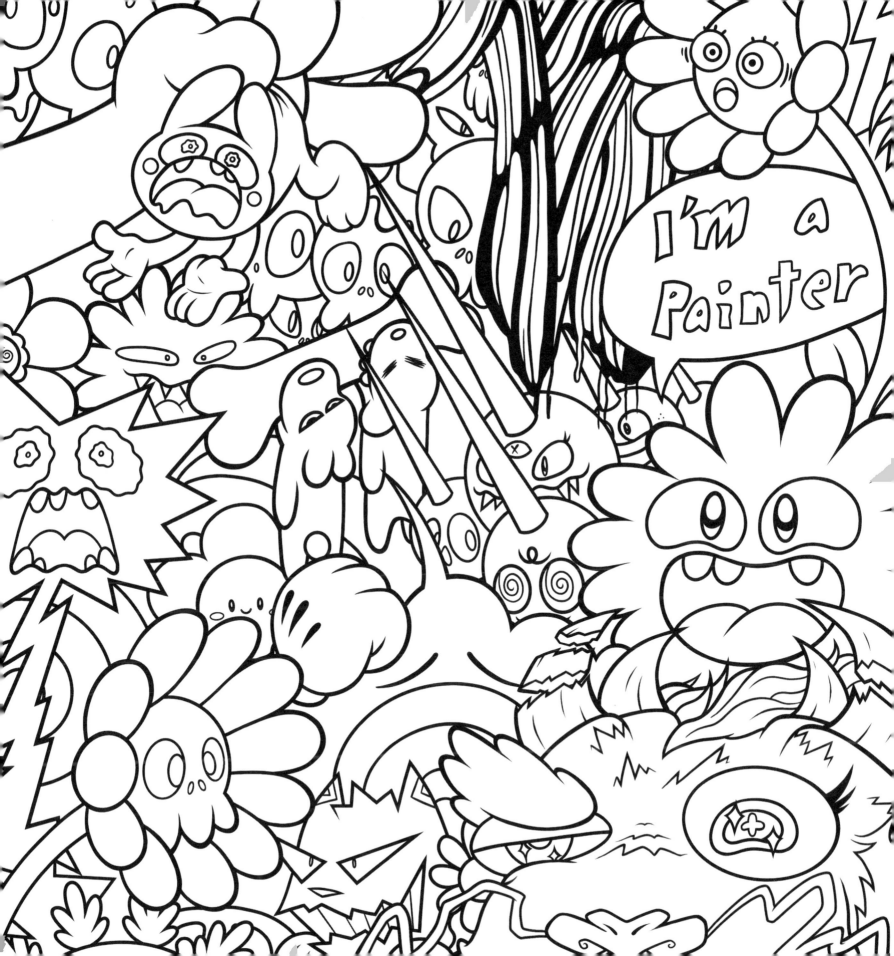

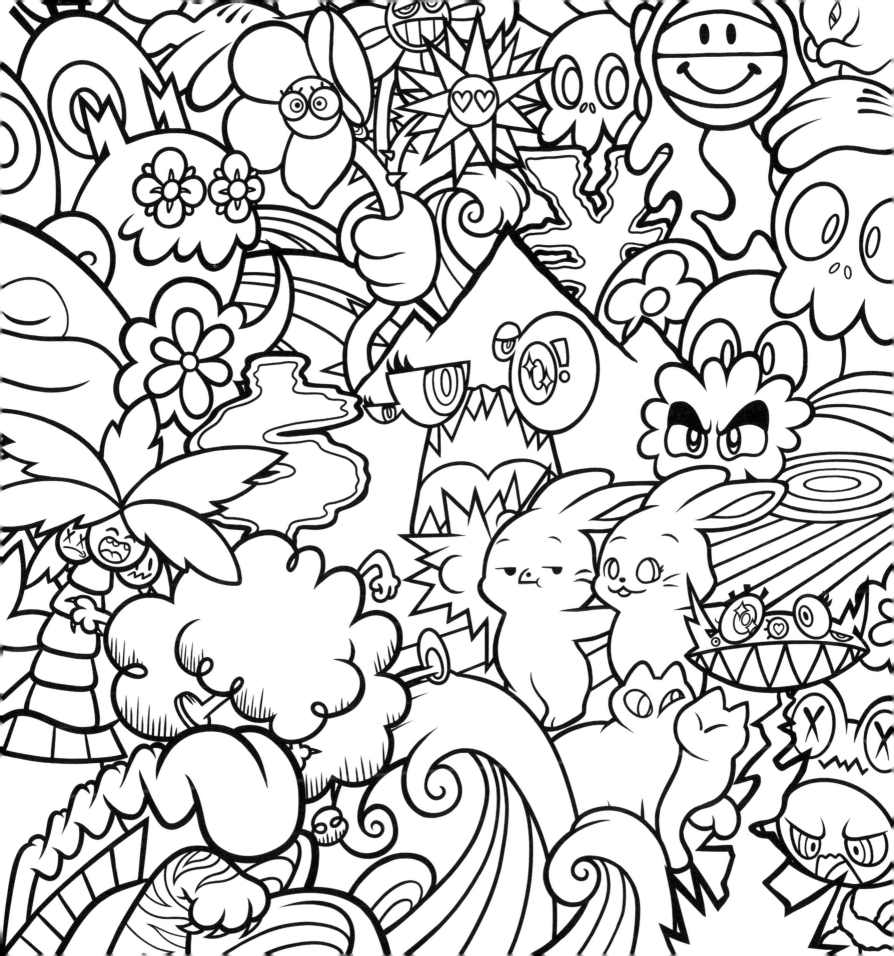

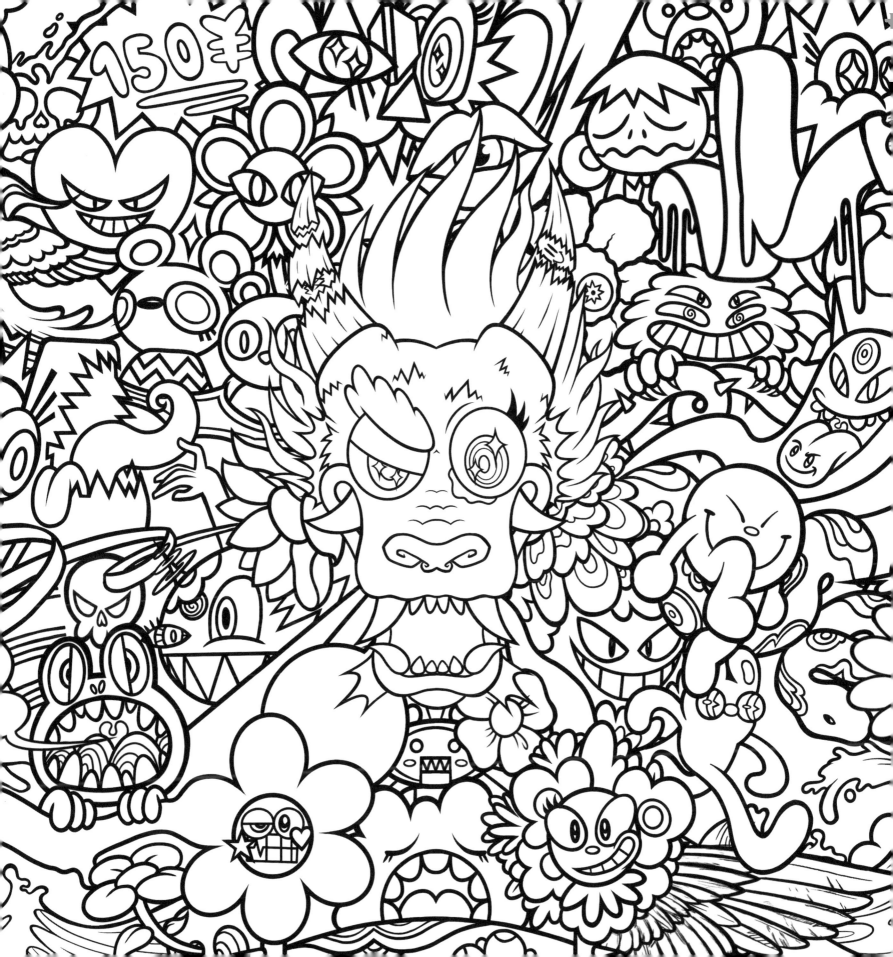

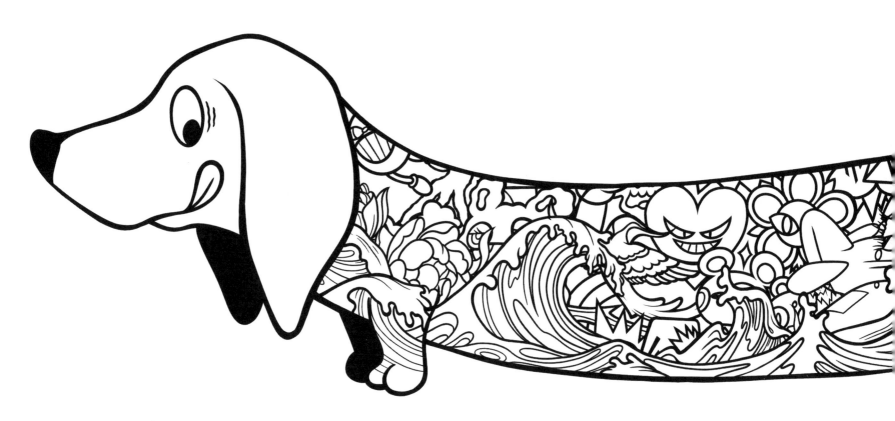

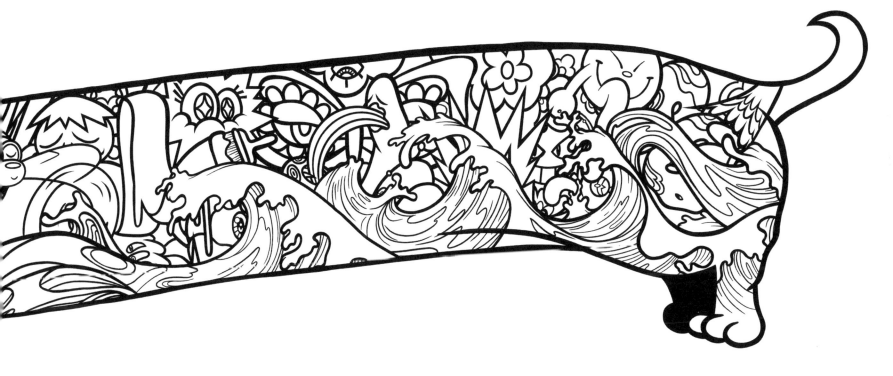

you did it!

you've reached the end of this wild, colorful journey.
I hope these pages brought you as much joy, laughter, and
unexpected doodle escapades as they brought me in creating them.
Now, as you close this book, remember that your imagination
knows no bounds. Let the colors of your creativity splash beyond
these pages and into every aspect of your life.
Whether you're scribbling, doodling, or just coloring outside
the lines, keep that playful spirit alive!
Thanks a million for being a part of this coloring extravaganza.
Don't forget to share your masterpieces with #Doodletopia,
and as always... Keep Creating!

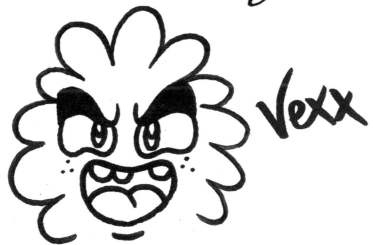

Vexx

ALSO BY *Vexx.*

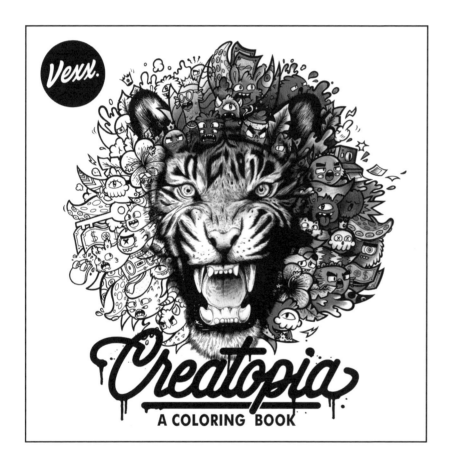

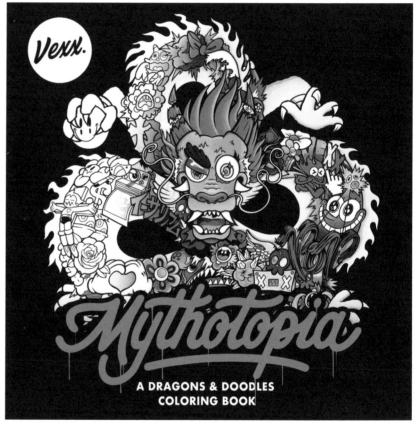

tarcherperigee